CW01003880

Pearls

*Advice for the
Path of Spiritual Awakening*

KEN MELLOR

First published in Australia
by Biame Network Inc., 2005

Copyright © Biame Network Inc., 2005

National Library of Australia Cataloguing-in-Publication data:

    Mellor, Ken.
        Pearls : advice for the path of spiritual awakening.

        ISBN 1 920892 79 6.

        1. Meditations. I. Title.

    158.128

Cover painting by Elizabeth Mellor
Edited by Bronwyn Collie
Cover and text design by David Constable
Production by Publishing Solutions, Australia
Printed in China

Biame Network Inc.
PO Box 271,
Seymour, VIC 3661
Australia
www.biamenetwork.net

Background

Ken Mellor is a master of meditation. Beginning in the early 1980s, he and his wife, Elizabeth, engaged in an intensive process of deep personal transformation through regular contact with two Indian Masters: Swami Krishna Gautam, a Tantric Master who lived in Australia; and Thakur Balak Brahmachari, a Vedic Master who lived in Kolkata, India. Ken's and Elizabeth's training was rigorous and demanding. Their primary goal throughout was 'full awakening'. This time – about four-teen years in all – was wonderfully healing, releasing, expanding and enlightening.

From early in the process, Ken and Elizabeth were encouraged to teach and to initiate people into the approach they were learning, which they did by combin-ing what they learnt from the East with what they already knew from the West. They have continued to do so for over twenty years, developing an international network along the way. Their approach, which they call Urban Mysticism, is a practical form of spirituality designed for people living in the modern world.

Ken has a unique talent for engaging people that usually enables him to know what they need in order to progress. The depth and breadth of understanding he brings to every encounter are strongly influenced by his extensive background in a variety of fields. Among other things, he has worked as an insurance clerk, social worker, university lecturer, psychotherapist, counsellor, trainer of psychotherapists, writer, parent educator, business consultant, personal and business mentor, and management trainer. His wide background enriches his understanding of people and their spiritual needs and processes. These days he devotes most of his time to teaching meditations (involving basic to advanced spiritual practices), acting as a spiritual mentor, and writing.

Ken has written several books of his own and shared the authorship of several others. He has also written for international professional journals and has contributed to newspapers, websites and magazines. His work has been translated into at least nine languages. Ken's and Elizabeth's most recent publication, their fourth book on parenting, is called *Teen Stages: How to guide the journey to adulthood* (Finch Publishing, Sydney, 2004). In both that book and *ParentCraft: A practical guide to raising children well (2nd Ed.)* (Finch Publishing, Sydney, 2000), they discuss many practical and spiritual approaches that they recommend for the process of raising children from conception to adulthood.

Acknowledgements

My greatest thanks go to Elizabeth, my wife. We have travelled our shared paths for twenty-four years now – learning, growing, evolving and awakening together. She is my life companion and soul mate, and a gift to me of wondrous proportions. I tested each of the 'Pearls' in this book on her and always got what I needed, responses all the way from delight, through bafflement and incomprehension, to tactful suggestions about how or where what I had written needed modifying.

My thanks, too, to all the spiritual Masters who have variously guided, supported, initiated, taught, mentored and loved me while fostering my spiritual awakening. Much of what I put in this book arose because of my relationships with you – from your teaching, your examples as I watched you at your 'work', and through your direct impact on me. I have listed you in the order in which I encountered you and not in an hierarchy that indicates the significance of your impact on me: Swami Muktananda, Adam Davis, Swami Krishna Gautam, Thakur Balak Brahmachari and Mother Meera. I have not included many others masters of various practices in a variety of fields to whom I also feel great gratitude; their contributions were not directly relevant to this book, though they contributed greatly to my development in other ways.

My thanks as well to everyone at Publishing Solutions, particularly Elena Cementon, for the wonderful job they have done on the production of this book. Their advice and help, and their willing cooperation throughout the process greatly smoothed the path of it publication. Also, thanks are due to Tony and Nada Smark, and Mark Davis for their shared creativity in arriving at the inspirational title of the book.

A big thank you, too, to Stephen Karcher, Mark Davis and David Carman who read the manuscript and made many suggestions that helped shape what you now have in your hands. Bronwyn Collie similarly contributed to the quality and final polish of the book as editor and I thank her for her many suggestions. Last, my thanks to Kathryn Schofield (from the UK) for agreeing to my publishing her description of what she experienced during darshan with me. She eloquently describes one type of experience that can occur after regular spiritual practice lasting for years. What she wrote provides a beautiful and fitting end to the book.

Contents

Introduction

On 7 October, 1987, I wrote a memo about Mantra Meditation to people who were interested in regular spiritual practice. They were all members of the organisation that Elizabeth, my wife, and I had started just over three years before for the purpose of sharing information, providing support, and creating a mechanism for both general networking and promoting spiritual awakening. My intention then was to make writing these memos a regular practice. I wanted to share some of the insights that Elizabeth and I had found helpful when meditating and teaching meditation.

We had taught meditation internationally for six years by then and were repeatedly asked whether what we taught was published anywhere. It wasn't; however, the often-repeated question prompted me to think about how to get various aspects of our work into print. I thought that writing short memos was a small step towards reaching this goal and, given how busy we were, a relatively undemanding way of achieving it.

At the time, I had little idea of just how helpful the memos would turn out to be, how much I would enjoy the process of writing them, or that I would write them regularly for the next seventeen years! I was greatly surprised, therefore, when, a short time after sending out the first three, many people began to tell me that they 'really enjoyed' them, learnt a lot from them and often referred back to them. I was also delighted when told that some people were putting them up on places like walls and refrigerator doors so that they could reread them easily during the day.

As the years went by, these memos became highly valued within the network of people to whom they were sent. Even years after they were written, it seems clear that the messages, guidance, suggestions, symbolism and general style are as relevant and helpful as on the day they were written. They have a somewhat timeless quality, which after all is understandable, since they are about the 'timeless' process of using meditation for spiritual awakening. Over the years, I was asked again and again, 'Are you ever going to publish them in a book?' Clearly, the ultimate answer to that question was 'Yes', although until fairly recently I was not clear on when I would do it.

Interestingly, many people have also referred to the uncanny way in which the memos they were reading were 'perfect' for them at the time. They were convinced that these occurrences were much more than chance, or what we usually consider as chance, and were laden with another kind of meaning – with what is called synchronistic significance. It is distinctly possible that your picking up this book today is laden with a similar significance.

The Process

Mostly I wrote the memos when I was preparing our organisation's regular newsletter. Occasionally, I had spontaneous ideas and would write a memo there and then, very occasionally doing several at once. Whatever the beginnings, when writing I would meditate quietly, holding the people for whom it was intended and the next memo together in my awareness. This was usually a holding of 'vacant space', because I often had no idea about the subject of the next memo at that point. While sitting, I would cultivate a light, still, open, receptive and expectant orientation; then, when I began to have specific ideas, or when something vague though promising seemed to emerge, I would make a few notes. The memos usually emerged from these.

Both the themes and the way to present them often occurred simultaneously. Sometimes, however, it was only the theme that occurred to me. I would then construct a story around it, or search my own experience to find an incident I could recount by way of illustration. Very occasionally, I told stories from others, or adapted their stories to the theme I was exploring.

Usefulness

I was very glad that so many people found the memos, or 'Pearls' as I now call them, so helpful. At the same time, I was repeatedly surprised by the frequency of comments such as, 'How do you know so accurately what I need to read?' or 'I usually find they teach the lesson I need to learn right when they arrived', or 'They always seem to arrive just when I'm struggling with what they're about'. A common variation on these themes was, 'Oh, I picked up one of your old memos the other day and it was exactly what I needed to know at the time'. Significantly, the implication was almost always that I was somehow monitoring these people's lives and writing specifically for each of them, a process about which they seemed hopeful, sometimes expressed gratitude and often experienced a little wonderment.

Occasionally unusual powers were attributed to me to try to explain these experiences; for example, that my intuition was highly developed after many years of meditation. However, I think that the causes of my apparent prescience were usually much more mundane and down-to-earth, perhaps to do with my developed sensitivity and frequently a lot to do with the way events unfold amongst people whose lives impinge upon each other. Moreover, people often experience occurrences as far from chance, because they have a meaning to them that both flavours their understanding and imparts a sense of a 'higher order involvement' in what is unfolding. In any event, to me it seems clear that whatever I did tapped into the non-linear flow of spiritual meaning called synchronicity, as seen in many readers' responses.

Sources of Inspiration

My life kept me in close contact with many people through the workshops, meditation sessions and other training events that Elizabeth and I ran. As a result, I was usually keenly aware of the kinds of issues with which people were grappling in their everyday lives.

Second, citizens of the world tend to face many similar issues at particular times. Globalisation of the media and the exponential increase in international travel are only two factors in the modern world that expose us to many common, personally significant themes: Scarcity of money, famine and worries about war are examples. Third, a spiritual path involving regular practices of some sort takes practitioners through many predictable stages during which they are faced with issues and challenges characteristic of each stage. Writing about these was therefore likely to resonate with anyone going through those stages.

Accordingly, familiarity with the issues people were facing in their lives, remaining informed about world events, and drawing on my experience with what people need as they evolve spiritually were all likely to contribute significantly to what I chose to write.

At the same time, as already mentioned, prior to writing a Pearl I would 'tune in' to those for whom it was intended, sometimes to specific people and sometimes to everyone on the planet. By meditating with open expectations on what was needed at that time, I was inviting the consciousness, lives and needs of those people to impact me and influence my inspiration and choices. I also thereby opened myself up to my higher consciousness so that it would influence me to write what was needed more generally at the time. You could see what I did, therefore, as a conscious attempt to divine what was important for my future readers; it was a systematic process by which I did my best to make what I wrote as practically helpful and spiritually awakening as I could. As it turned out, although I didn't know what I was doing at the time, my approach was also a means of making the synchronistic field between the Pearls and their readers, both past and future, as significant as possible.

Why 'Pearls'?

Pearls are created by nature through a wondrous process that converts an irritant or intruder into something beautiful. Oysters (or mollusks) 'breathe' the sea in which they are immersed. The water flushes and cleanses their systems and feeds them. Now, even though many of us are not aware of it, all of us also live immersed in an 'energetic' ocean, the Universal Ocean of Awareness. This is a reality to which both advanced souls through the ages and an increasing number of today's scientist have attested. We 'breathe' the Transcendent Waters (or Energies) of this Ocean through our systems in order to flush, cleanse and feed ourselves, and we do this every moment of our lives.

Life being what it is for oysters, they occasionally get stuck with a grain of sand or some other foreign material inside them and, despite their best efforts to flush out or expel it, the intruder stays lodged in place. And, life being what it is for human beings, we also get stuck with material foreign to our nature, material that we need to flush out or expel, but cannot dislodge. Such intruders will cause trouble if we don't deal with them in some way.

This is where pearls come in or, to be more precise, pearl-making. To take care of their problem, oysters secrete an iridescent substance that slowly surrounds and isolates the intruder. This coating builds up over time until its opalescent, glowing beauty is a wonder to behold. In this form, pearls nestle safely within oysters, their original form no longer any cause for concern. Thus what starts as a cleansing or protective measure, ends with beauty.

Applying the chapters in this book to ourselves is a similar process. The suggestions are all designed to help us to deal with challenging aspects of ourselves, our lives, our subjective experiences and those aspects of our histories with which we have become caught. These challenges require an effective response from us or we are likely to contract in the face of Life and interrupt its flow through our systems. Living day to day will then becomes much more difficult. Also, contracting and interrupting Life is highly likely to thwart our efforts to realise greater Awakening. By using the suggestions offered here, however, we are able to take 'material' that causes disturbances to normal processes of living and Awakening and transform it into wonderful assets whose beauty we can celebrate and use as inspiration to continue on the path.

Written for people who are interested in Spiritual Awakening, the chapters focus or concentrate on what we need to do to progress spiritually. Areas covered include the profound contribution Spiritual Masters can make to our progress and on various aspects of Masterhood itself. The chapters, or Pearls, are designed to offer guidance, to illustrate and, hopefully, to illuminate. They are designed to show how to make pearls out of common irritants and challenges in the lives of those dedicated to Spiritual Awakening. They also explore some characteristics of Masters and Masterhood, various aspects of our relationships with Masters and, perhaps most importantly, how to engage in and persist with practices designed to release Master Processes within ourselves.

Importantly, each Pearl can speak in many different ways, particularly if you allow yourself to dip into the book at random. There are distinct advantages to not reading the Pearls in order. Allowing our intuition or just 'plain chance' to lead us to what we read has for thousands of years helped release the synchronistic forces that are at work in our lives and given us a chance to learn from what they offer us.

What Masters Are

All of us are masters in many areas of our lives. When we have mastered some process, skill set or the like, we can do whatever is required under normal circumstances without even noticing that we are doing it. Think of activities such as putting on your shoes, driving a car, or eating. We do many things like this without giving them a thought, except when things don't go smoothly.

Masters in a spiritual sense are people who are similarly accomplished in the area of spiritual practice. For example, I am a master of some forms of meditation, particularly the ones that I teach; and there are many other masters in a wide variety of spiritual 'schools' who have mastered a vast array of general approaches and myriad specific practices within those approaches.

Some Masters, usually as a result of long-term devotion to their practice, are evolved and expanded personally to a significant degree. When we are with Masters like this, they have a profound affect on us, simply through the impact of their presence, let alone when they actively engage us in some way. Those people whom we are told have mastered as much as it is possible for human beings to master are called Enlightened.

Importantly, even after spending only a little time with significantly evolved people, we are likely to notice that events seem to unfold with more purpose and that they impact us more strongly, as if they are orchestrated by some hidden plan. These Masters' attunement to the higher reaches of consciousness and their conscious participation in the subtle dimensions of life clearly seem to enable them to invite us into a synchronistic field, so that even mundane events can take on distinctive and previously hidden significance.

I guess it is obvious that only very few people reach such exalted heights as Enlightenment and that most of us are still walking the long road to get there. These Pearls were written as aids for various stages of your journey, aids that offer ways that can help you to consolidate, expand and realise your spiritual mastery. They each contain pearl-making processes by which you can meet many of the challenges of your journey and turn them into beautiful assets to brighten and enliven your life.

Responses

Judging by the prolific feedback Elizabeth and I have received over the years, the Pearls have made a significant contribution to the awakening processes that many people have experienced. They have liked the simple stories, found particular Pearls inspirational and discovered that they came to understand themselves and their practices more deeply through what they had read. Many people also liked to ponder or meditate on each Pearl in order to discover their many levels of meaning.

Whether they had just read the Pearls or had read them years before, a large number of people commented on their timeless relevance. This is very gratifying in a world in which people are encouraged to dispense with, to lose interest in or to regard as no longer useful anything that is not the latest model, is not seen as superceding well established ways of doing things, or is simply not different enough from everything else.

In our modern context, the wisdom of the ages is automatically suspect to those who are indoctrinated with the belief that the 'old', the 'established', or procedures that have been 'proven for years' automatically means that something isn't worth considering. At the same time, merely offering advice doesn't make it good advice, so having a way of sifting it before following it is useful.

Suggested Approaches

This is a book for you to dip into, not to read like a novel. You could also simply flip through the pages to allow 'chance' to guide you synchronistically to what you need to read; or you could ask a question that captures the essence of the guidance you seek in order to 'magnetise' yourself to invite the pages you need to read to open under your eyes.

However you get to what you read, the style of each Pearl is designed to stimulate a pause in your normal ways of approaching things, a pause pregnant with the possibilities of new insight, new direction, new commitment to ways of acting that seem to hold more promise than what you have done before. The style can also help you to recognise and recommit to what has already worked well for you.

I recommend, therefore, that you read in a way that allows and promotes contemplation. Make at least a few additional minutes available for this, both while you read and afterwards. Do what Stephen Karcher, the well known author of books on the I Ching, says: Take what you read and 'turn and roll it around in your heart-mind'.

Using this approach helps us intuitively plumb the depths of ourselves and the various forces impinging on us in our lives as they relate to what we are reading. The special meaning and significance of the Pearls is then much more likely to arise spontaneously.

While contemplating, let understanding and insight arise, rather than trying to analyse your way into them; analytical or linear thinking can obliterate the subtle yet profound lessons we may find in each Pearl. Open up, relax and give yourself to the effects on you of what you read; allow these effects to impact you; allow yourself to look into your unknowing and your knowing, and to see what is there as it actually is; listen to the themes and messages you get from your reading and what they are saying to you; feel the significance of your reactions. Allow all these things to guide you to the understanding and insight you need.

You will know when you have digested what you have read and that it has nourished you fully when you have a sense of completion. Even if you don't initially see clearly what is important, which you might; even if you don't hear the guidance that you want acutely, which you could; even if you don't feel that you understand completely yet, understanding that is more than possible for you; continue to allow your inner processes to do what is needed, which they will. Simply give your inner processes time to do what they need to do – minutes, hours, days, weeks. In the end, you will know and understand what is important for you.

Capital Letters

Throughout the book you will find the first letter of some words capitalised. I have done this to draw important distinctions that become obvious as we progress in awakening, distinctions that are not always obvious while we are not yet Awakened. The 'capitalised words' refer to states, experiences and qualities that are far beyond the day-to-day. So, for example, Love (with a capital L) refers to Divine Love, a Love that so far transcends the everyday as to be indescribable, while love (with a small l) refers to feelings of love that we can experience under normal circumstances; similarly, 'Life' refers to the Source of the Energy that enlivens all living things and transcends them, while 'life' refers to dimensions or aspects of living that are usually obvious or available in the world; and 'Master' and 'Mastery' refer to people and their levels of realisation that are far beyond normal worldly experience, while 'master' and 'mastery' refer to normal day-to-day usage and experience.

Unfolding Process

Finally, I want to mention the transition in content and style through the book. Because I have presented the Pearls in the order in which I wrote them, the patterns of interest and emphasis that I and others had through the seventeen years of their creation emerge naturally as you read. In my experience, these changes of emphasis and understanding reflect a common occurrence when people engage in spiritual practices over many years.

The center of our interests changes; the emphasis we need to put on different aspects of our lives, both inner and outer, changes, too. Sometimes these changes are sudden, and sometimes we evolve through them so gradually that we could easily miss them.

Whatever your experience is, my hope is that you will realise the wonderful balance and completion that arises naturally out of any form of sustained spiritual practice, a balance and completion reflected in the sixty Pearls available to you here. I also hope you will discover a guiding hand behind your efforts that leads you to exactly what you need.

One thing is certain, your path will be unique and, provided you persist, a cause for celebration. I hope these Pearls will help you on your way.

Ken Mellor
Seymour, Victoria, Australia
April 2005

Blue Pearl Meditation

When the blue pearl appears in meditation, it is said to be an auspicious sign of the approach of high levels of Awakening. The meditation here uses the image on the previous page and is designed to promote this result.

It is important that you understand that the painted image is an external representation of what you may see in meditation; it is not the real thing.

Step 1: Sit upright in a comfortable position. Look around you and see what is there; listen to the sounds around you; notice what you are touching and what is touching you; and notice any tastes or smells coming from around you, too. Do this for at least half a minute, and for longer if you have the time.

Now, also become aware of your inner sensations. You may feel them as physical experiences; hear them as inner sounds; see them as colours, images or pictures; or taste or smell them inside you in some way. Relax into and accept whatever you experience as you do this.

Step 2: Now turn to the blue pearl (on the previous page). Concentrate on it, keeping it in the center of your awareness as you do. Importantly, allow yourself to see it, rather than trying actively to look at it. Let the blue pearl shine towards you; allow it to reach your eyes on its own; and let it shine into your eyes, reaching into you through your eyes as it does. Simply open yourself to seeing it.

The blue pearl will stimulate you. Notice and accept whatever you experiences as it does: any thoughts, feelings, impulses, desires, memories … (Return to Step 1 if you need help to digest any responses.)

Step 3: Keep doing Step 2 and start to look at the blue pearl through the area between your eyebrows. It is as if your forehead has become transparent there; so see, feel, hear, touch, taste or smell the blue pearl through there. As before, notice and accept whatever you experience while you do this.

Step 4: Now as you continue with Step 3, allow the blue pearl to absorb and digest you, so that you become part of it; or allow the blue pearl to come into you, so that you digest it and it becomes part of you; or both. Open yourself to whatever your experience as you do this.

When you are ready, stop what you are doing and bring yourself back to your normal awareness of where you are.

1
Mantra Meditation

(Mantras act as tools, catalysts and vehicles for Awakening. Often understood solely as, for example, a way of occupying the mind, or of inducing hypnotic states, many Mantras enable us to produce far more than these kinds of relatively trivial results. Mantras help us to access and to harness the Life Force available within us; they help to re-engineer our connections to our Selves; and they actively and directly promote Awakening.)

Once you are initiated into using a Mantra, everything becomes a meditation, provided you use it. So it makes sense to practise awareness of the Mantra in everything you do. Many benefits flow from doing this, particularly as you dedicate yourself to practising your meditation throughout your day-to-day life.

The Mantra is always repeating. It is in everything, in every moment. It is the bridge you can cross at any time into the Wondrous Fullness that is available within you. It is your means of selecting the channel from which you can be continually flooded by Fullness from within.

1

You have the nectar, balm and aliveness of the Master Energy in you. By repeating the Mantra and being aware of the repetition that is independent of you in each moment of your day, more and more of the Grace of this Energy will flood you. Your experience of everyone and everything will then gradually transform.

Simple practices can help you to develop an on-going awareness of, and oneness with the Mantra. All help to keep reminding you of the Mantra as you go through your day. For example, you could spend a few seconds being aware of repeating it and of its independent repetition each time you do some everyday thing, such as eating, showering, lying in bed before sleeping, cooking, writing letters, or before driving the car. Some people use timers to remind them to repeat the Mantra at regular intervals. There are many such simple practices.

Whatever method you choose, start with one that is easy for you to use. As you master it, expand what you do a little at a time by trying something different. In this way, you can quickly find that you are repeating the Mantra almost all the time, whatever you are doing. Many people are pleasantly surprised at how quickly doing this produces a continuing awareness of the Mantra.

As a further hint, when you repeat the Mantra, remember to have a double orientation. The first is to repeat the Mantra actively to yourself by seeing, hearing, or feeling it repeat, or by saying to yourself. At the same

time, you listen, look and/or feel for the automatic repetition that is always there. Often surprising at first,
most people find that the Mantra is indeed repeating in
everything and that they can notice this repetition at
the same time as they repeat it voluntarily.

A wonderful flooding of Grace occurs each time you
match your repetition with that other, automatic one.

2
Take Root in the World

Your life here in this world is like living in a garden and you are a plant in that garden. The earth is below; the heavens above. The beauty and life in the garden result from the interaction of heaven and earth. When thinking of your life like this, it becomes obvious that you need to take root in its day-to-day events, for these form the earth in which you are planted.

In fact, your Complete Realisation relies on your fully taking root in the world like this, so embrace your daily affairs in celebration of their contribution to your growth. Every worldly act draws more nourishment into you from the everyday things in your life and pushes your roots down further.

So nourish yourself every day: Do the dishes, write your letters, drive your car, raise your children, do your work, visit your friends, paint your house, love your dear ones. Live fully. Moreover, make sure that you do the practical worldly things that demand your attention. Remember always: Every worldly act contributes to your full flowering.

Naturally, the question arises: 'Do certain tasks produce the best growth?' And the answer is: 'The best ones are those immediately awaiting your attention.' In other words, deal with what is confronting you. You will see, hear or feel them right there before you. Even the things that don't seem particularly related to promoting your worldly and spiritual growth are doing just that.

A magnificent sense of timing and delicacy operates in relation to the events of your life. The result is that precisely the right demands for promoting your essential growth are being made on you each day. By being aware of and available to these demands and opportunities, you will do exactly what is necessary for your next step. So take the step that is at your feet. At the same time, avoid trying to take steps that you haven't yet reached.

Simply get on with what is at your feet and I am sure you will find the fastest shortcut is in the route under your feet.

Celebrate the world. Notice its beauty. Contribute to that beauty by being active in the world. The fragrance of your full flowering will then spread everywhere and transform everything you touch. And at exactly the same time, all you do will transform you, too.

3
Nourish the Plant
Meditate

In the garden of your life, you are a plant. And it is vital that you nourish this plant. Plants need sun, air, minerals and other earth-borne ingredients, and they need water. With these nutrients they flourish and grow. Without them, they wither and die.

Inside you, your worldly being has the same essential need for nourishment.

Now, the true Master is at one with the Source of this nourishment, with Life itself. And every day you, too, need the unique Nourishment that Life offers. So make yourself available to Life every day through using the practices the Master has given you. Doing so is very worthwhile. More than this, it is fundamental to living fully in this world.

Such a practice means spending some time every day in meditation. Meditation is a powerful way of releasing Life's essential nutrients in you. Through meditation you can experience the inner light, breath, showering and completion of your own Divinity.

So repeat your Mantra. The way you do it is up to you. Perhaps you will sit or lie for some time each day. Perhaps you will meditate as you perform certain tasks. Perhaps you will make every moment of the day a deliberate act of meditation.

The essential thing is to meditate in order to absorb the Light, the Breath and the Showering that are essential to your inner Being.

The more you meditate regularly, while living fully in the world, the greater will be your rewards. Vitality, lustre and harmony will arise in you more and more.

You will arrive at a full, breath taking flowering and your fragrance will spread everywhere. Others will delight in your presence and will want to be with you to experience your increasing Grace and Strength, and to savour your developing Sweetness and Beauty.

Another thing helps, too. Spending time with the Master catalyses this wonderful process, because the Master's on going inner Nourishment sets off the same processes in you.

4

The Master Is the Gardener of Your Divinity

True Masters are the gardeners of your Inner Being. Your uniqueness can find its fullest expression in their care. And your Ultimate Fulfilment is intimately woven into the direct experience of your unique Being-hood.

You can think of it in the following way. The fully grown plants of our Divinity start as tiny seeds. Masters take us into their Divine Gardens. At the optimal moment they germinate us with Initiation. They then tend us, nurture us, guide and prompt our growth, and keep the garden around us in optimal condition.

Compared to the Masters' gardens, normal life is a desert. The Masters' gardens are true paradises in which every need can be satisfied, everything fulfilled.

Masters lovingly and gracefully cultivate everything in their gardens. They cultivate the whole of you – the Being of you. They see much more deeply than you the overall plan and balance of life and its impact on you, and they cultivate accordingly. They know when to act and when to wait. They know when to tie you to a stake to back up your strength and uprightness, and when to release you to your own devices to test and develop your own strength. They know when to shelter you from the elements and when to release you to deal with them yourself.

To get the full benefit of their availability, you need to remain open to their tending. While doing this, celebrate their availability to you. Open yourself actively to the Nourishment they provide in every thought and action they direct towards you. Allow yourself to be Cultivated by them.

The choice is yours. Of course, you can also choose to try to make yourself unavailable in some way. And because Masters will not force you, this may seem to work. However, once you are Initiated, wherever you go lies within your Master's garden. All our Masters continue to watch over us, waiting for the time when we call again to ask to become a willing participant in the life, relief and fulfillment that comes from their direct attentions.

And there is another perspective: The inner reality, not known to many people, is that true Masters have no choice. Whether or not they pay obvious attention to you, they cannot separate from you. At the deepest levels, they are connected to you forever. After all, the Master in you is You.

5

Do You Notice the Master on the Beach?

Have you ever watched sea gulls at the beach? You will see them doing many things. Some will be soaring on the wind, some floating on the water, some walking on the sand at the water's edge, some fossicking further up the beach.

They are generally alone, engaged in their own activities with a beautiful intensity and calm. But produce some food and gulls come from everywhere, wheeling, swooping, running, scuttling, chasing, squawking, fighting, escaping, returning, pecking, and giving up or winning the prize.

And if you observe closely, you will notice a peculiar thing. The birds show virtually no awareness of the person feeding them. They are far more intent on the food – the food leaving the hand, the food in the air, the food on the sand, the food almost in another bird's beak, the food in the possession of another bird, the chase, the attack, the defence …

Yet paying even a small amount of attention to the person feeding them would show them a lot. Rare are the people who simply spray the food around in all directions. Mostly, they tend to distribute it in a particular way. Some people tend to feed the quiet, relatively calm birds in preference to the rowdy, fast-moving, combative ones. Others reverse this preference. Some give to the weak; some to the strong. With even a little observation, the birds could place themselves to take advantage of such patterns.

And another peculiar thing – the gulls seem frightened of and so avoid the person doing the feeding. One and all give the person as wide a berth as possible. If the food falls close to the feeders, the birds will dart in and dart out again as quickly as possible. Often they are so intent on the darting that they miss or drop the food anyway. And if it falls too close even for this manoeuvre to retrieve it, the food may simply sit untouched on the ground. Yet, in all likelihood, no one has ever tried to harm one of the birds. They would be perfectly safe to stand at the feet of the feeder, and even perch on an arm or a knee, where they would be far better fed than the rest of the flock.

So remember and learn from the gulls: To be truly fed, you are best to notice the feeder, not the food or the others being fed.

6
The Right Advice

A Master gathered his disciples around him one day and said, 'I've noticed in recent times some practices to which I want to draw your attention'. He paused as they settled down to listen. 'I've observed all of you giving and taking advice amongst yourselves.' He paused again. 'Have you thought about what you're doing? Why is it that so many of you are giving others directions on what to do?' No one seemed sure what he meant and all stayed silent.

'It seems curious to me that any of you would think that you are ready to give advice. Do you yet know who you are, the Being from which you arise? Do you yet know the Truth about your Origins and your Destination? I look at you and I listen to you talking and I wonder what all your talk is for.' Still silent, some of the listeners were remembering times when they had attempted to guide others with more confidence than their experience had warranted.

'You seem like children when they first go to school. Some vie for the top position by talking with assumed authority, or by trying to help others in the way they

have seen their mummies and daddies do it. Some
seem to think that imitating the teacher makes them an
instructor, or they act as if the same advice works, like
a rule, regardless of the situation or the people
involved. Others simply make something up in order to
have something to say.'

'But what do you actually know yet? Even the knowing
you think you have could be as distorted as the image in a
flawed mirror, or the sound of a warped record, or the
working of a faulty appliance. And you will not know
whether it is distorted or not. In giving advice to each
other, I know you mean well, that your intent is pure and
loving. Yet, even with that intent, you are accidentally
spreading distortions, warps and faults. You're inviting
those you advise to be as flawed as you by looking into
your mirror, becoming warped by using your record, or
by applying your faulty instruments to their projects.'

The Master paused for a time and then said, 'My heart
goes out to you all, for I know you wish to share the
benefits you are experiencing. So if one of you will ask
me, I'll demonstrate the best advice to give.' After a few
moments, one of those present said, 'What is the best
advice to give?'

Everyone was extremely attentive to everything that
followed, for the Master's message had moved them all
greatly. Afterwards they all agreed that no matter how
hard they had looked, how carefully they had listened,
or how delicately they had held on to what was happening, the Master did not seem to respond in any way.

7

The Master's Fuse Connects You to Your Potential

Every person is born with the full potential for Enlightenment. Very few realise the Nature of their potential. Even fewer Realise the amazing fullness that is in their Divine Potential.

It is as if you were born as a beautiful new house. You contained every modern electrical appliance, some were familiar and some you had never seen or heard of before. Everything shone brightly. Every part of the house was balanced in a wonderful harmony of space and form.

The power was available. Everything was ready to do its job. And, while over the years you learnt to live well, you did not know that everything was working worse than it could, some was not working at all, and that your life in this house could be very different.

Then one day you meet a Master who Initiates you.

Suddenly, everything inside you, everything in the house, seems different. All sorts of new things start to happen. There are lights and sounds you have never seen or heard before. The white cupboard in the corner of the kitchen makes a humming noise, a light goes on when you open the door and the inside gets cold. Then too, in the living room against the wall, that strange, three-dimensional work of art starts to glow red and get hot at times. And where at night you always had to use candles, you now find some rooms are permanently lit.

Everything is different. And your life fills up with unexpected excitement and challenge.

Always watching and never actively interfering in your experiments, the Master guides you to all sorts of new discoveries by suggesting various experiments you have not thought of. Each discovery makes something easier. You learn more and more. Food in the 'white cupboard' keeps longer. The 'work of art' keeps you warm on cold nights. The bumps on the wall panels turn lights on and off.

'Why', you wonder, 'is everything working so differently now?' And gradually you understand: Your makers could make you perfect, but could not provide the fuse to connect you to the power supply that lay dormant within your reach.

The Master's Initiation put in a fuse that connected you to your Power. His subsequent guidance helped you to discover how to claim that Power and live it fully.

8

The Master Is the Power, Your Hand Is on the Switch

Like an infinite supply of electricity, the Master's Grace is available to all his or her students and disciples. Whatever varied capacities they have, there is always more than enough to empower their Full Aliveness.

The Master's intent is to saturate everyone with Grace, to activate their very Foundations, to activate Life Itself in all. Freely and lovingly, the Master expresses a heartfelt desire for everyone's Ultimate Fulfillment by making Divine Realisation available to all twenty-four hours a day. This availability is guaranteed.

The outcome of the Master's availability is very much up to the recipients, however. You can live with increasing intensity by making yourself increasingly available to his or her Divine Energy, or you can diminish its effects on you by ignoring it.

Your deliberate choices are crucial. While the Master is a power supply, your hand is the one on the switch and you control the intensity.

To switch on, you have to be attentive to the Master's lessons. Look when the Master shows you something; listen when the Master speaks; feel when the Master touches; notice when the Master says to notice; act when the Master suggests you experiment. The attentive ones are switched on.

To turn up the power, you do things to help and support the Master in the world. Just as the power station, giving power to lights, can be lit by those same lights, so you can contribute to your Master. And then wonderful things happen. The nature of what you do opens you more to that aspect of the Master's Grace. And what you open up to floods through you after first having been enlivened many times over by the Master. If you make light available, you will shine more brightly. If you make love available, you will radiate and melt with more and more love. If you make time available, all the time you need will be there for you.

What you dedicate becomes a routine and abundant part of your own life – and very much more. As you shed even a little light for the Master, the Master offer Full Illumination and Enlightenment to every part of you.

9

As the Roots Spread, the Tree Can Grow

Asked one day to explain the relationship between Masters and devotees, the Master said, 'We need each other in all sorts of ways. The Master's manifest presence in the world is like the branches, trunk, and taproot of a tree. The tree above the ground is in the heavens, the taproot is driven deep into the earth below. So the tree links heaven and earth.

The Master's devotees are like the extended root system of the tree. Just as the roots spread out into the earth in all directions around the tree, so devotees live in the world around their Master. They form a link to the world for him through their lives.

'You may not know that trees always live and grow in relation to their roots. The roots spreading out into the earth enable the branches to spread just as far. This causes a beautiful mutuality to exist between the tree above and the roots below. Also, the size and strength of the tree above is directly dependent both upon the spread of the root system and how well it draws what the tree needs from the earth.

'At the same time, the tree feeds the earth below it. Anything that drops from it becomes part of the earth on which it falls. And because all that falls has been exposed to the heavens, the tree feeds the roots with heavenly refreshment and vitality. So you can see that the tree feeds the earth from the heavens, at the same time as the roots feed the tree from the earth.

'Added to this, the life of the tree depends both on its place in the light and on its capacity to harness that light. Light is essential to its life and to the life of its roots. In other words, light is life to the tree. Very importantly, if the tree dies, the roots die, too. So the same light is life to the roots as well. Severed from the tree, the roots can only wither away, yet, while linked to the tree and driving further and further into the earth, the roots grow in strength and capacity.

'Now notice the parallels. Our mutual fulfillment comes from our connections through the Tree of Life. So just as I affirm my link with you as my roots in the world and feed you with the fruits of my Meditation and Realisation, you can affirm your link me as the trunk and the branches and freely feed your goodness back to this so they grow in strength and stature. The tree can then flood you with more light and spread even further afield for everyone's benefit.'

10
Three Shop Owners

Three shop owners came to the Master one day. They wanted him to tell them which one he most favoured. The first said, 'I had my shop before you initiated me. It all came from my hard work and nothing is changed from that day'. The second said, 'I started my shop on your advice and you have advised me at every step. I celebrate my blessings by tithing. I started with one and now I have twenty shops'. The third said, 'I had my shop when you initiated me and I started a new shop shortly afterwards. But, although I love you and show you this by tithing, everything has gone wrong. I'm now worse off than before I met you'.

The Master said, 'You are all confused. First, put one way, I don't favour any of you. Put another, you are equally favoured. And most important of all, you are equally responsible'.

'First, your shops are like three branches on a tree. Imagine that I am the roots of this tree. I feed all my branches as fully as I can with the Life energy available to me. Only the capacity of the branches can limit how much of this energy flows into them. So understand this: All I can supply, I do supply. How each of you use this is up to you.

'Second, you're like gardeners who tend your branches, using me as a consultant. Whatever my advice may be, it's you who is responsible for what you do to your branch. The first of you is very independent, never accepting volunteered advice, nor asking for any. What guidance I might give would be unused, so I stay silent. The second of you benefits from seeking advice and taking it into account in his decisions about what to do. The third one of you asks much but notices little. He is like the first in wanting to go his own way, like the second in wanting advice that will make his business prosper, and like himself in the way he mostly reacts against what I show or tell him.

'Understand what I'm teaching. I love all of you. Each of you is benefiting according to his capacity and his need. I am responsible for feeding you in the way I do and for the advice I give. At the same time, each of you is responsible for what you do in response to me. Also, even if you don't know it, each of you is learning to realise a Unique Profit.'

The Master lapsed into a meditative silence for quite some time. Then suddenly he opened his eyes, stood up, hugged them all and said with a smile, 'Remember, all of you, the main business I'm helping you to run is the one in which "the Realisation of You, your inner Self" is the profit. This Profit will go with you forever, whereas all your shops and worldliness will not'.

11
Surrender
Hold Your Hand in the Flame

'Look at the flame', the Master said to the group sitting with him near a blazing fire. 'Surrendering to the Master is sometimes like holding your hand in that fire.' He paused to let what he had said sink in. 'This is particularly true when something important to you is being challenged. I want you to think about that carefully. What would you have to do to hold your hand in the fire?'

'It takes great dedication and a determined act of will to do it.' He fell silent for a few minutes, allowing those gathered around him to ponder what he had said. Then he said, 'These are essential parts of surrender: Dedication, action and will.

'Just imagine it. To do something so obviously damaging as putting your hand in a fire would take great dedication. The intensity of that dedication would need to be at least as great as the intensity of the "apparent danger", at least as much as the anticipated cost.

'Instinct is completely opposed to such an act, too. Your normal reflex would be to pull your hand back the moment it began to feel the heat. So, to overcome this, you would have to do something very powerful to keep you hand in the flame. You could not just happen to do it without thinking about it. It would be no accident. You would have to decide to act.

'You would need to use a continued act of will, too. Every moment with your hand in the flame would require a re-affirmation of the decision to keep it there. Otherwise, your natural instincts to preserve yourself would take over and you would wrench your hand away.

'So how is this relevant to the Master Process? Well, the Master's presence includes a Distilling Fire that touches every part of you. Some of this is very pleasant and immediately affirming. You welcome it. You can easily go along. Surrender in these areas is easy at these times. Some of my affect is much more of a challenge, however, for it is as if I am urging you to damage yourself by putting your hand into a fire. To place at risk what you hold dear, particularly those aspects of yourself without which you don't think you can survive, requires a determined act of will.

'Surprisingly, though, when we brave the potentially damaging flame we perceive, we discover that the Master's Flame only ever sustains Life. It can only ever create, heal, support and distil everything into Life.'

12
Swimming in the Stream of Life

Standing on the banks of the Ganges with a flooding torrent cascading past, the Master and some disciples were watching a boat being swept along by the raging water. Suddenly it overturned, throwing its occupants into the water. Hours later, after finding the sole survivor miles down stream, they were sitting around a fire.

'There's something to learn from this incident', said the Master. 'Think of Life as being like this river. It always heads to the ocean – always – and carries everything with it. Like this river, it sometimes has a wonderful power, a beautiful strength that sweeps all along with it. At other times, it is much more tranquil, showing a much more benign majesty in its progress, even meandering along at a sedate and easy pace.

'Now think of the people who fell from the boat. One immediately started to swim frantically for the shore, while another, for some unknown reason tried to swim directly against the current. Both were quickly exhausted by their efforts and sank from sight. Then there was the one who seemed to realise the futility of fighting the current, who, nevertheless, also exhausted himself by fighting to keep his head above the water. He thrashed around with his arms and kicked vigorously every time he seemed to be sinking.

'Finally, there was this one', the Master nodded at the survivor. 'Tell us how you survived.'

'Well, I almost didn't for a while', he began. 'The current was incredibly strong and there was such turbulence I thought I would surely drown. So, like the others, I struggled. But every time I struggled, I went under – every time. Yet every time I kept myself relaxed and flexible, bending as the water bent me, sinking as it sank me, coming up again as it bore me up – I was fine. I quickly found that it was always best to give myself to the speed and direction of the current, to forget my own immediate goals. In fact, at the end, I was enjoying myself. But eventually I was feeling too tired to last much longer. At that precise point, I was carried to the shore and was able to climb out of the water easily. It was as if the river knew I needed rest when I did. You can see how far it carried me by the hours it took all of you to catch up to me.'

'Perfect', said the Master, 'swimming in the steam of Life is managed best just like this'.

13
Desire

Desiring it,
I seek it.

Having it,
Fulfils it,
Leaving me desireless of it.

By fulfilling desire,
I learn of desirelessness:
The ease, the quiet, the light of it.

So then,
Within desire,
I desire the desireless.

While desiring the desireless,
I affirm desirelessness.

Then, when that desirelessness is affirmed
I realise 'I am that':
The Sublime.

14
Do What You Are, Be What You Do

The Master and a group of disciples were sitting in a large garden one evening. The sky was clear and the atmosphere still carried the fresh tang of recent rain into the balmy night. The Master was lying languidly on the floor as his feet were massaged. There was a pervading peace.

Suddenly there was uproar as a harried looking man, filled with tension and worry seemed to catapult into the centre of the group. The Master, still relaxed and lying down, watched with a glint in his eye. The others all sprang to their feet and, becoming increasingly agitated, began talking to the new arrival and each other. They strove with each other to get everyone's attention. They shouted at each other and tugged at each other's arms and clothing. They seemed completely unaware that the Master, now sitting up, was there. Confusion reigned supreme, until eventually the Master began to speak.

'There is uniqueness both in each thing in creation and in the events that unfold around us. This uniqueness is expressed and revealed in every moment of being. Nothing needs to be done for you to find it. There are no special ways to act. No striving is involved. No special thoughts or feelings are needed. The uniqueness of everything simply is. Learn to act out of that uniqueness.' He paused a moment, then added, 'Do what you are; Be what you do'.

Then he turned to one of the women present and said, 'Bring me a large bucket of water'. Shortly afterwards, when he held the bucket in his hand, he said, 'Now watch'. And he emptied the water onto the ground at his feet. Some of those around him were confused, unclear what they were supposed to do.

Noticing the puzzled looks, the Master said, 'Watch the nature of the water. Forget the rest. Just watch the way its "waterness" is expressing itself right now – without effort, striving or thought. That bit is flowing away; that bit is seeping into the ground; that is puddling; and that is softening the small obstruction holding it back'. He laughed and clapped his hands with delight as the little pile of earth at which he had pointed subsided below the surface of the water. Then he lapsed into a meditative silence, while obviously remaining alert to what was happening at his feet. When the only thing left was a moist stain on the ground, he roused himself, looked intently at those around him and in a voice so quiet it was almost a whisper, he said, 'Just so, find the "I Am" of you – and live It; avoid making a commotion about things'. Then he turned on his heels and walked briskly away.

15
The 'I Am' of Getting What You Want

'Everyone comes seeking help with something', said the Master one evening after seeing many people that day. The Master was still fresh, light and relaxed.

Hundreds had come asking for help with all sorts of problems, projects and hopes. Some were sick, some dying, some wanting a business venture to prosper, some to find a mate, some seeking help with family members, and only a few to find 'Spiritual Awakening'.

Each received a uniquely suitable response from the Master and went away brighter, easier, fresher, quieter. They left with renewed faith in the Master's backing. 'I do what I can to satisfy them all, but most don't understand the real point of my help', she reflected.

'What do you mean, "the real point of my help"?' asked one of the small group of helpers with her. 'You give them all something. They know they can come to you for anything and that you will give it to them or help them to get it for themselves.'

'Ah yes', she said, melting their hearts with the glowing warmth in her glance, 'but how much easier it would be for all of you, if you would be the "I AM" when cultivating awareness of what you want'. Everyone was confused – they had not heard of this before.

'When you ask me for help with something, you think that you are asking me. But I'm merely a doorway to the "I AM" inside each of you that is the Source of your own creativity. When you ask for something, I make the "I AM" in which I am centered available to you by lifting you into that State as much as you will allow. Yet what I do for you, you could do for yourselves. Moreover, any capacity you think I possess is already available in you.

'Understand this: My purpose with each of you is to help you live your own lives fully, to show you what is possible for yourselves. At the same time, I don't want you to rely on me. This is very important because you can claim for yourselves the capacities you see in me. I'm not here only to do things for you – nor can I succeed unless you agree. I don't force anything with you. Yes, what I do makes a difference, but your participation is crucial. And you'll only ever benefit to the extent that you are available and committed to it.' She fell silent for a while, then roused herself.

'The fundamental secret to learning to fulfil your desires for yourselves is to be the Abundance, the Life, the Light, the Symphony – to be the all encompassing creativity of the Life in you. Being the "I AM" makes all things possible. So experiment for yourself next time you want something and discover how right I am. To do this, repeat your Mantra to heighten your awareness of "I AM" and hold what you want in your awareness. "I AM" and what you want will be with you there and then.'

16
The Three Cs of Getting What You Want

'You told us some time ago that the secret of getting what we want is "to be the 'I AM'" as we think of what we want.' The statement, from a man, red faced with anger, was clearly an accusation. 'Yes. That's true', the Master replied mildly. The man thumped his clenched fist on his thigh and spat, 'Well – it doesn't work!' 'Oh?' queried the Master, 'What happened? I take it that you have tried'.

'Oh, I tried alright. But nothing happened. I have money trouble and need something to happen very quickly. So I was thinking about my troubles and repeating the Mantra, as you recommended, and nothing happened – except that I got even more worried. If anything, since then my money worries have worsened.' He was still very upset, but seemed slightly calmer.

The Master got to her feet and began to walk slowly backwards and forwards in front of him. She seemed to be thinking deeply. Her pensive silence aroused his curiosity – and calmed him down even more. He seemed to be just about to speak to her again, when she spoke.

'It's great that you tried to do it the way I suggested.' She looked warmly at him, a loving softness in her eyes, as she went on, 'It seems to me that you got everything right and, with a very minor correction, you should get the results you want'. The man looked baffled and cncouraged at the same time. 'What you need to do', the Master continued, 'is to use the Three Cs of getting what you want'. 'The Three Cs?' several people exclaimed in unison.

'Yes: "Conceive", "commit" and "celebrate"'. She poked the air with an upraised index finger as she said each one. 'First, you conceive, that is, imagine the way you want things to be. Imagine that everything is perfect and, most importantly, imagine that this perfection exists now. Second, you commit to this image by deciding that this is the way things are and will be. Having committed yourself in this way, live as if your image is true by acting in ways that are consistent with it – even small ways are enough. Be total in your image and total in your commitment, and be sensible in what you choose to do. Third, celebrate from then on the reality of your original image or conception. With joy, gratitude and happiness, notice how everything is changing to what you want, and notice the things that are already what you want them to be. Put aside the past and celebrate as you live out your commitment to your conception of how you want things to be.'

She then turned to the man and said, 'You were doing
all three. You conceived that what you did not want
was true; you were committed to its truth and lived as
if it were true; and you celebrated, by expressing passionately all you could find that fitted your image'.
Here she paused for effect, nodded to some of the others who were listening intently and added, 'And the fix
you're in shows us all how good you are at the three
Cs'. She smiled to soften the message. 'All you need to
do is concentrate in exactly the same way on what you
want. Let go of what you don't want. I'm sure you'll
succeed just as well.'

Within a week the man was back. He was all smiles
and told the Master how beautifully his financial affairs
had begun to work out within days of using the three
Cs on what he wanted.

17
Blow on the Flame, Not the Smoke

They had all had a busy day. It was winter and cold and windy – an ideal time for a fire. The Master asked for one to be lit. Several people volunteered and got to work. The Master, meanwhile, busied himself with arrangements for the evening meal and the program to follow. After a time, it became obvious to all that the fire lighters were in trouble. Smoke was billowing into the room – the wood was clearly green and damp.

Much of the trouble arose because the fire lighters were waving their arms about and blowing at the smoke to attempt to get the smoke to go up the chimney and away from themselves. This only made matters worse. Their eyes were streaming and they were coughing and spluttering.

The Master, after pretending not to notice for a while, finally did something. He got one of the fire lighters to pick up a 300 millimetre square piece of cardboard, to hold it horizontally and then to move it vigorously up and down close to the smouldering wood. Almost immediately flames were dancing as the wood burnt strongly and everyone began to warm up.

'Let's consider what happened earlier this evening', said the Master during his evening talk. 'When I asked for a fire to be lit, we got more smoke than anything else. The principle seemed to be "Where there's smoke, there's fire", and we were given as much smoke as possible, perhaps on the grounds that "The more smoke there is, the bigger the fire". He paused, smiling delightedly at his joke. 'As you'll all have observed, it takes very little fire to cause a lot of smoke. If you are familiar with these things, you will know that we usually get most smoke when a fire is first lit. Because of this, the best thing is to get a fire burning as strongly as possible, and as quickly as possible, because the hotter the flame, the less smoke there is. Also, the secret is to blow on the flame, not the smoke. You'll have noticed how quickly things changed when this is what was done.

'If you think of your awakening as the flame and the release of your denser energy (you might say "impurities") as the smoke, you'll understand something.' He sat back for some minutes to give them time to think about this. 'Do you see what I mean?' Another pause, then he continued, 'What you put your energy into is what you get in life. If you concentrate on your troubles and difficulties, then you'll quickly be surrounded by them, just like the smoke. But if you concentrate on the Refining Fire, which is stoked strongly each time you meditate, the flame will quickly be so hot that everything will burn with the maximum of heat and the minimum of smoke'.

He paused again: 'So in your lives, blow on the Flame, not on the smoke'.

18
We Are All One of God's Rainbows

They were all in the living room one spring afternoon.
The Master had been closely watching several rainbows
produced by the sun shining through a teardrop-shaped
crystal hanging in the window. The colours were brilliant – beautiful. A whispered conversation had developed between several people on one side of the room.
The Master had affected not to notice, although, as
time passed, their conversation grew louder.
Eventually they began to hiss noisily to each other, the
result of their efforts to express their frustrations and
not to disturb the Master. At this point, the Master
raised an eyebrow and asked what was going on.

The dam burst. A current political conflict was the
cause. Two sides had formed and all involved had
entered the fight. Each side accused the other of being
wrong, of not understanding and of having started the
problem. Even as they were explaining, they began to
again, with each asserting that the other side should
take the initiative to resolve the dispute.

Suddenly the Master demanded tersely, 'What causes those rainbows on the floor?' His tone immediately caught their attention. 'The sun', one replied. 'Go and look at them', he said. No one moved. 'Now!' – he shouted. Shocked at his apparent anger, everyone jumped to comply. When they were at the window, he asked evenly, 'What colour is the light from the sun?' 'White', several people answered. 'Exactly', he said. 'Now, look back at the rainbows.' They all did. Then they waited.

'Those rainbows are produced by the sun passing through that crystal hanging in the window. Each colour – red, orange, yellow, green, blue, indigo, violet – is in the white light. It's as if the crystal displays for us the different colours in the light. Moreover, the sun shining through different coloured crystals would produce rainbows with different hues. The basic colours would be the same, but the intensity of the colours would be different.

'Now imagine that God is the sun, the whole cosmos a giant crystal. All the beings in creation are then easily seen as individual crystals of different colours. With God's Light shining through them, they produce God's rainbows. At the same time, all the different rainbows combine to form the Great Light of God, in which each one has its unique part to play.

'So realise this: People's qualities and behaviour are like the colours in each rainbow spread on the floor over there, the worldly rainbows that show the unique light that arises from God's Light shining through each person.

'From now on, always remember that, we are, each of us, one of God's rainbows, part of God shining in the world. Look at those colours. None is right and none is wrong. Each of them simply is. You would be better spending your time finding God's light in yourselves, and in everyone and every thing else, instead of arguing and criticising. And remember the contribution of the differences. Each colour is necessary for the rainbow to be complete. God includes all that is. As we realise the Ultimate, we realise the completion in this and the contribution each aspect makes to All That Is.'

19
Leave the Slipstream to Do Your Own Driving

'What is the best thing to do?' the Master was asked one day. 'I don't know whether to give up everything and come and live with you, or whether to continue living as I am and visit you as much as possible. I can see for myself that what I've been told is true: Those who live with you seem to progress very rapidly and easily.'

The Master looked at the questioner meditatively for some time before answering. 'There's really no best thing to do. Whatever you do will have its advantages.' The corners of his eyes crinkled as he asked, 'Do you drive a car?' It was well known that this young man was a driving 'fanatic'. He loved driving his car as quickly and as competitively as he could. 'Yes I do!' he exclaimed. The Master laughed, then the young man laughed, too, just then noticing the tease.

'Okay, then, consider this analogy. You know how a vehicle travelling at speed down a freeway has a slip-stream, an envelope of "thinner" air behind it which seems to suck other vehicles into it and drag them along.' His listener nodded knowingly. 'Then you certainly also know that it takes much less power to drive in a slipstream, because the power of the leading vehicle creates the "hole" in the air that sucks you along.' 'Of course', was the reply.

'Well then, imagine the Master is a large truck driving swiftly down the freeway. Living with the Master is like travelling in a slipstream for long periods. Visiting the Master is like travelling in a slipstream for shorter periods. Whenever you're in the slipstream, you'll be learning; whenever you're out of the slipstream, you'll be learning, too. What you learn will be different in some ways and the same in others. Just remember the difference between driving in slipstream and driving out of it.' Another pause. 'What's certain, though, is that "slipstreaming" is never enough.' The young man was surprised at this.

The Master paused again to allow the young man's surprise to settle. 'To Realise truly, everyone has to do their own driving. They have to be able to drive fast enough and long enough, too. The Master's realisation may carry you far further than you can go alone, and perhaps do so more quickly, to begin with at least. But your own Realisation is what matters in the end. When you drive through the gate to your own Masterhood, no-one will be up ahead. You'll be "on your own". Your own Developed Capacity is all you'll have.

'The answer to your original question, therefore, depends on the style of contact you need to have in order to develop a Master's capacity as quickly and easily as you want to develop it.'

20
Surrender, Don't Give Up

The Master and a group of four people were lying casually on the lawn one afternoon, enjoying the mild, spring sun. The sky was a clear blue. The air, fragrant with blossoms, still carried a hint of winter in the slight coolness of the light breeze. All were very relaxed. After a while, the Master rolled over and asked one of the women to go and make tea for them all. His request was met with a deep, disgruntled sigh and a surge of petulance as the woman stood up.

'What's the problem?' the Master asked. 'Well I was really enjoying being here and I don't want to go inside and make tea for everyone. But I feel caught.' The woman stopped, looking decidedly uncomfortable and uncertain about what to do next. 'Caught?' the Master prompted lazily from his reclining position in the sun. 'Yes caught!' she exploded and then spoke in a tense rush. 'I feel caught because I have to be surrendered to you and if I'm not surrendered to you then I won't get the benefit of being with you, and yet you often ask me to do things I don't want to do, at times that are inconvenient to me; and I feel as if there's something wrong with me that I don't jump up and do everything happily and willingly in the way I see all the others doing things; and then I think that you know all that is going on inside me anyway and I feel ashamed that I'm not surrendered...' She fell silent with a helpless shrug.

The Master gently pulled her down to sit in the grass beside him. Then he sat up so they were sitting oppo site each other. 'Will you do an experiment with me?' he asked. The woman nodded – and then crinkled her brow ruefully as she realised she didn't know to what she had just agreed. He said, 'Arm-wrestle with me'. She was surprised, but willingly got onto her stomach and took his hand as he did the same.

'Start', he said, and they both pulled and pushed at each other for a while, until the Master said, just a little sharply, 'Surrender!' Her hand fell limply to the lawn under the weight of his arm. 'Start again', he said. So she did. After a brief struggle, he repeated his instruc- tion, 'Surrender!' Again her hand fell straight to the lawn.

With that, he looked her in the eyes and said firmly, 'Don't give up. I said, "Surrender!"' The woman looked extremely bemused. So he said, 'Let's do it again, and this time you tell me when to surrender'. So they started again. When she said, 'Surrender', the Master kept the pressure up, but instead of continuing to push against her as he had been, he twisted his wrist and pulled her strongly into a beautiful embrace. And there they nestled for a while, enjoying the different joining of their strength.

Eventually, the Master smiled and said, 'I've just surrendered to you. Real surrender is to do with availability.' Then, still smiling, he went and made the tea.

21
Make Your Leaving a Way of Joining Together

From a distance, a man who had been with the Master for several years could be seen gesticulating at him. Almost shouting, but just managing to control himself, he said, 'Well I'm going. It's time to move on. You've taught me all you can and it's time I did my own thing. What I think is important to me, and I don't know how you think I can learn if I don't go out and try my own hand at things'.

'That sounds good to me', the Master replied mildly.

'I mean', continued the man, 'I've benefited enormously from what you've taught me over the years. It's just that I don't think you've been right all the time and I know, I just know, that I have to go and work things out for myself!' He became increasingly agitated and red in the face as he spoke. As he struggled to talk calmly, he clenched and unclenched his fists.

The Master replied, still talking mildly, 'You seem to be acting as if you have to convince me, or as if you have to fight me to say all this'.

'Well that is how I feel!' the man retorted. 'And I think that you'll think badly of me for wanting to do things for myself and that you'll reject me in some way if I spend less time with you.' Vulnerability cracked his voice despite his efforts to sound angrily assertive.

The Master reached out, took his shoulders in his hands firmly and shook him lightly. 'Pay attention to me for a minute. This is me here. With me there is no fight – even though you've been thinking there is. Everything you say you want to do, I agree with. I've been urging you and all the others to do this the whole time I've known you. I urge you always to test things for yourself, to understand that others cannot live your lives for you – only you can live your life. I've helped to build your inner strength and to help you live in that. I've respected your opinions and have contributed mine so that you will expand your understanding, just as I have learnt at times from what you have taught me. I have done all this to promote your autonomy and Masterhood. I celebrate with you that you are wanting to do all that you have said.' He had been speaking firmly and now softened his tone. 'I will miss seeing you, if you spend less time here. And I support your desire to spread your own wings.'

'But I have to do it myself! What else can I do?' the man almost shouted again.

'Well, first of all, I repeat, you can stop fighting with me', the Master replied. 'That is not necessary. The fight is inside of you, not with me. To live your own life, you simply live your own life. For you to be right, others don't need to be wrong. For you to leave, you don't have to find fault in those you are leaving, nor do you need to imagine that they are finding or will find fault in you. Make your departure a celebration. We each have a unique contribution to make – sometimes together, and sometimes not.' The Master stopped talking and looked at the man searchingly.

'Go out into the world and as you do, make your leaving a way of joining together. By doing this, you will learn more; and in that way, our strengths and who we are will be available forever for us to share with each other and with others, too.'

22

Realisation

The Beginning, the Middle and the End

In the beginning comes excitement and hope.

In the middle comes familiarity, disillusionment
and persistence.

In the end comes Fulfillment
And a new beginning.

By making the end the beginning
And the beginning the end,

All is One.

Practise.

23

Get into Your Own Driver's Seat

The Master sat in meditation, a serene expression on his face. Others were getting on with their daily tasks. One young man stood out, however, because he kept looking long and hard at the Master. As the time passed, it was clear from the young man's flushed face and jerky movements that he was becoming increasingly impatient the longer he had to wait.

As soon as the Master came out of meditation, the young man rushed across to him. 'It's all so easy for you', he blurted out. 'You sit there in meditation, enjoying every minute. Every day you look wonderfully serene and balanced, as if nothing troubles you. I wish I could live like you. But I don't think I ever will. I try so hard to be like you. I do all that you have told me. I sit the way you sit. I walk the way you walk. I act the way you act with people. I spend time imagining what's going on inside you and try and make these things happen inside me.' He fell silent, looking very dejected, then added with a sigh,

'But it's just so difficult and I don't seem to be getting anywhere'.

The Master looked up at him warmly, reached for his arm and sat him down next to where he was sitting cross-legged on the floor. 'Your dedication and all your efforts will pay off. You've been learning all sorts of things while you've been doing what you've been doing.' He paused briefly to think, then continued with a twinkle in his eyes. 'You're like someone trying to drive a car in the wrong way. It's as if you've seen others driving their cars and like the look of it and all the things they seem to be able to do by driving, but you haven't yet learnt how to drive properly. You show this by your continued attempts to drive in the way it looks to you from the outside – what you described as sitting the way I sit, walking the way I walk etc.'

Again the Master paused, then nodded to himself. 'A way for you to understand what you're doing is to approach it differently. You've been so desperate to drive your own car that you have been complicating things by actually trying to drive it from the outside, instead of the inside. It's as if you're driving by clinging to the steering wheel through the driver's window. Obviously, this is an almost impossible position from which to drive. It's a tribute to you that you are doing so well.' He paused again. 'Think of this analogy and do the obvious.' The Master stopped. The young man looked puzzled.

After extended silence, the Master continued. 'What would you do if you saw someone actually driving like this?'

Still looking puzzled, the young man said, 'I'd get the person to stop, open the door, and get into the driver's seat.'

'Precisely', the Master said. 'Now you do the same. The door is your heart. The driver's seat is "I AM". So take your own advice. Stop what you're doing and realise "I AM" in your own heart. Get into your own driver's seat and everything will be much easier.'

24
God Is Innocent of the Charge

A troubled couple said they wanted to speak to the Master. He, wanting them to be at peace, immediately made himself available. 'What is it that you want to discuss with me?' he asked when they were all comfortably seated. The couple looked at each other, uncertain about how to start. 'I suggest that you just start. If it doesn't come out the right way, you can always modify it by adding something later', the Master said. He looked at each, encouraging them to speak, and then waited patiently.

'It's to do with your increasing concentration on religion', the woman began. 'When we first met you', the man continued, 'you rarely mentioned anything to do with religion. But now you're doing it more and more. I don't want to get mixed-up in anything to do with religion; that was one thing we enjoyed about coming to you in the early days. I've had all sorts of bad experiences with religion'. The woman took up the discussion. 'You talk about God, the Ultimate, the Divine

Principle and all sorts of things these days. And when you do, I cringe inside.'

In response, the Master asked, 'How is this a problem? You are free to come or go'. 'We know this', the woman said, 'and we don't feel constrained by you in any way, and we see the benefits in being with you. Besides, I suspect that I would be better to come to terms with my difficulties with those sorts of words'. She smiled self-consciously at her partner and then at the Master. Both smiled back.

'Yes – I see wisdom in this', said the Master. He paused and then explained, 'As our real Awakening progresses, we come into closer and closer contact with our personal Divinity. Each of us is that Divinity, so this increasing closeness is important to understand. Moreover, how can God be avoided, if our progress is real? God, for that is the name of our Divinity, is the origin of All That Is. So God is our origin too. As we realise Oneness with our Source, it's more and more relevant to discuss it and how to promote our further Realisation of it.'

'But', burst out the man, 'all sorts of people mouth off about God. The word is meaningless, a confusion, an excuse!'

'No, no, not at all', said the Master soothingly, 'God is innocent of these charges'.

'The God that can be Realised within is real and true; Realising God in this way is the only true religion.

There is only Reality in this religion. Many people have made many mistakes in relation to God. These mistakes have affected others, sometimes drastically. But the word "God" is not responsible for any of these mistakes or your difficulties; it has simply become associated with them in your experience. On the contrary, the word "God" is a powerful Mantra that attracts to all that use it the attributes of God, or if you prefer, your Source, or the Ultimate. Try repeating it. Make friends with it. You may find, as others have, that by doing so you discover an open door into your deepest Being.'

25

When the Recipe Works, Use It

'How did you do it?' the Master was asked. It was a relaxed time for everyone. All the chores of the day were completed. The fire had been burning brightly since the early morning, so the room was warm and comfortable. Dimmed lights and soft music added to the peaceful atmosphere. 'How did I do what?' he replied. 'How did you learn all that you know? I'm amazed at how much you know. When I compare what I know with your knowledge, I feel like I know so little.'

The Master looked both alert and puzzled. 'What is so important about what I know? What I know is useful to me; but to you, it is only useful to the extent that I can use it to support your efforts. It's primarily what you know that's important. I think that you'd be better concentrating on your own realisation, rather than on the realisations you think I have.'

This young man had a pattern of wanting things quickly and easily. He had once said to the Master that he wanted simply to come and sit with him and imbibe all the necessary learning without effort. Remembering this encounter, the Master now said, 'You already have in your hand everything that you need for your Full Realisation. I and others have already given you this. Keep using what you have and you will reach your goal. There's no substitute for your doing this. No-one else can do it for you'. He paused then added with emphasis, 'Remember this! Only you do the realising; only you can do the Realising'.

'Sometimes we eat for pleasure – perhaps even a lot of the time. Whether for pleasure or not, we always have to eat to stay alive. The same is true of our "inner" development. We can do a lot of what promotes Realisation for the pleasure of doing it, because there's much pleasure in many of the practices. But the pleasure is not the purpose. The prime purpose is to Realise Oneness with God – through Realising "I AM", our own Godhood. This releases Ultimate Aliveness. We need to make "feeding our souls" one of our highest priorities'. He paused for emphasis. 'The consequences of this kind of eating are Cosmic.'

'As I said, you already have in your hand all you need to know: Your meditation, your orientation to feelings, your commitment to the Beauty in every moment – all the basics I and others have taught you. This is your program, your recipe. And note this well. Part of that recipe says, 'Use this recipe every day for the rest of your life – no matter what!'

'But I've been doing it for so long now. I want it without the effort', the frustrated young man interjected.

'Now just listen', the Master said firmly, 'You asked. This is your answer. The recipe works. How do you think I have Realised all that I have. I was given my recipe long ago and I wanted to eat, so I used it. I still use it, too, because I collected another recipe along the way that I've used ever since. It reads, 'When a recipe works, use it.' Success comes to those who do this.'

26
The Beloved

'When we are in love, everything is beautiful. Our bodies throb with that melting warmth that softens and enfolds, inducing, almost irresistibly, the desire to enfold the beloved, to merge and to blend completely. Living to be together always – every separation is keenly felt and only lived through by entertaining thoughts of how wonderful the next reunion will be.

'When together, all seems complete. When apart, everything takes second place to the desire to be together; all thought turns to reuniting. When in love, things that were once important, become secondary – food, work, the other routines of life. What do they matter beside the consuming desire to find completion in the beloved once again?

'We live to look, to hear, to touch, to taste, to smell the beloved. As we look, we see only beauty, we see behind the petty interferences of daily life to the very core. We see the beloved's radiant Being – Love, Light and Life – qualities released by the Natural Flow running its course. Every gesture, every word, every part is so fragrant and sweet. The excruciating pleasure of being with the beloved is sought above all else. And we blissfully endure it at every opportunity.

'This astounding love', said the Master, 'is a pale reflection, a poor replica of the Love we can experience in God'. He was alight and alive as he spoke. Living what he was saying, he seemed to radiate light in all directions, his voice was resonant, strong and soft. He was shaking mildly in the passion of his words.

Those gathered around were deeply moved – and curious. 'How can we experience this, if we haven't yet met God?' one of them asked for all, 'Where is God?'

The Master smiled, clearly remembering his own experiences. 'The thing that works, that is True, is to realise that you have always known God – your Beloved. Whatever your present experience, you loved God before. You simply allowed yourself to be distracted.'

'To unite again with God in Love, start by doing what you would to activate worldly love that has diminished. Start to pay attention to the Beloved again. Attention reawakens the Love. You may need to devote a lot of time in the beginning, time that will be needed for you to change your habits. But as you do, you'll find your Beloved waiting for you as He-She has always waited. Love expressed is always returned; Love shared always intensifies; so a Loving momentum will build quickly.

'Look into your heart. Feel your heart. Listen to your heart. Taste and smell your heart. God is in there, as are all the wonders of Rapturous Union with God. Open your heart with Love. Feel Love there, see it, hear it, taste and smell it. As you do, pour your fullest love toward the Spark of God in there and open yourself to it. In return, you will be flooded with such Love, such Gifts, that you'll scarcely be able to credit what is happening. Do this every day.'

27
Trust Your Heart, Then Use Your Head

'Trust your heart', the Master repeated – with emphasis. He was talking to a middle-aged woman about a family problem.

'But, what do you mean, "Trust your heart"? I've heard that sort of thing so many times and it seems important, but I don't understand it.' She was pleading and sounded frustrated at the same time; a look of desperation appeared fleetingly, until with an obvious effort she wiped it away. She continued, 'I know it's spiritual to "let your heart lead you", "let your heart guide you", "follow your heart as it finds the way" and such like. But I don't know how to do it'.

The Master said, 'I understand your frustration. I remember being in the same fix'.

After a long pause, he went on. 'However, I discovered that it's actually very simple. In any situation, to be guided by your heart, you notice what is going on in your actual heart as you live through or think about the events you are facing. Just feel, or hear, or see the sensations in there. You'll find that this releases a love-centred appreciation of the situation. Even if you're not feeling very loving at the time, love can guide your perceptions and conclusions as you do this, then you can better decide what to do.' The woman nodded speculatively.

'Think of your own life. You've described family problems to me. What you described seems complex and difficult, as if a lot of wisdom or understanding will be needed to solve them. It all seems so difficult, perhaps because you're trying to think them out too much, to understand them and solve them through rational analysis alone.'

The woman nodded her agreement. 'I have always been taught to think things through, to work out what is going on in advance and plan accordingly.'

'But it's not working, is it?' the Master said, and she shook her head.

'As I see it', he continued, 'this is because understanding can come from the head, while real appreciation comes when the heart and head work together. Learn to include your heart in everything. You'll come to trust your heart as you use your head. Involving your heart opens you to deeper truth than your head alone can reach, just as using your head opens you to perspectives and conclusions that you are unlikely to discover if you restrict yourself to using your heart'.

'Try it right now in relation to this family situation of yours.' She sat pensively for a few minutes, gradually becoming more at ease. After a while she looked much brighter. She said, 'It really works. I know what to do now. All along it was right there. The moment I noticed my heart, I started to appreciate what I'm dealing with. Before that my understanding was really limited, although it didn't seem that way at the time'.

28
Cook Your Own Cake

It had been a stimulating session for all concerned –
many questions, many answers, many new directions,
many new perspectives. While all the more interesting
for the variety of issue raised, a constant thread was
behind everything: How to become Fully Awakened.
At the end of the session, when all others had fallen
silent and most had started to drift away, an ardent and
dedicated young woman spoke quietly to the Master.

'I want to understand fully so I can get the most out of
all you teach', she said. She seemed to want the question to go unnoticed by the others present, most of
whom by then were taking refreshments or talking
amongst themselves. The Master called them back, saying, 'Listen everyone, this is important'. The young
woman repeated her question as they all gathered
around.

'My consuming interest in life is to find Ultimate
Fulfillment. So that I get the most out of everything
you teach us, I take note of all that you say to everyone
and practise as much as I can. But I seem to get myself
into trouble a lot.' She looked at the Master steadily, as

he adjusted his position while smiling at her gently.
'Go on', he encouraged. 'Well, I don't know what to do
about the contradictions in what you tell us. Just
today, you told us to "be assertive" and "be accepting of
what others do", to "put ourselves first", but also "to
serve others by putting them first", and other things
like that.'

In response the Master said, 'Imagine that you are in a
cooking class, and that you follow to the letter every
instruction given. On some days this might work out
well, while on others you might get yourself into a fine
old mess'. He paused. 'Imagine this: As your teacher
walks along the line of students he says to the first stu-
dent, "Put in more milk". To the second, he says, "Put
in more flour, there's too much milk in there". To the
third, he says, "That needs more raisins"; and to the
fourth, "That needs fewer raisins". The fifth and sixth
have their cakes in the oven. He says to one, "Take
that out straight away, it's already cooked"; while to the
other he says, "Cook that some more, it's still wet
inside".'

After a pause, the Master said, 'Notice that every bit of
advice is "right"'. The Master paused again to let what
he had just said sink in. 'What you've done is to listen
to everything and follow every instruction, as if everything was said to you alone. From now on, relate to the
reality of the situation you are in. There are many who
need advice and many who get it. Some will need more
milk, some less. Some will need more raisins, and

some less. Some will need to cook their cakes for longer and some will need to stop because they are already cooked.

'From now on, though, you just cook your own cake. Make the adjustments you need to make for your own benefit and stop trying to follow the adjustments others need to make.'

29

You Are Your Own Nursery

The Master sat with a small group. He was aware of the intense gaze of a young man who had not visited before. In his early twenties, his freshness and openness were appealing. Eventually, the Master asked, 'Do you have a question?' 'No', the young man replied, 'but I'm getting bored just sitting here. I like things to happen quickly'.

All seemed clear then, so the Master talked at a leisurely pace. 'These days we're accustomed to everything happening quickly. Life moves at a rapid pace. Our entertainments are taken on the run. We are busy, busy, busy. Even twenty years ago, the pace of life was sedate compared with today. We now have the habit of acting quickly, thinking quickly and expecting results quickly.

'I like this because these developments expand our consciousness in important ways. They loosen up the hold we try to keep on established way of doing things. In particular, I like the changes because in this modern era

we're learning how to promote Awakening rapidly.'
The Master paused, again taking in the intensity of the
young man, who reminded him of a sprinter about to
set off in a race. 'However, some changes and developments take time; they are not instant. This is true with
Awakening. We need to remember that Realising
Awakening involves us in a growth process – and this
growth takes time.

'Part of the meditative way is to wait actively', the
Master then paused for a long time to emphasise the
point he was making. 'Think of a seed', he continued.
'Once it is planted, we can do much to encourage its
growth into a fully grown plant. We can turn the soil,
fertilise it, support the plant when necessary and water
it. But then we need to wait for the necessary time to
pass for natural growth to assert itself, for only the seed
(and subsequent plant) can do the growing. It's the
same with people.

'However, many people, in line with the times, want
Awakening without waiting and without applying
themselves to the task of nurturing "the seeds". They
act as if all they need to do is go into to a nursery and
buy their plants fully grown, as if the plants of their
personal Awakening can come from someone else, as if
all that they have to do is to come along after all the
work is done by others and reap the rewards of the
other people's efforts, as if their own time and effort
are not necessary.

'However, each of us is our own nursery – a fact we cannot avoid. We need to plant the seeds of Awakening in that nursery, nurture them ourselves, and allow the necessary time for them to grow. Many benefits are available from experienced nurserymen or women. They have great knowledge, skill and experience that can help us with our own efforts. What is theirs, however, can become ours only to the extent that we apply it ourselves.'

The intensity in the young man's look now had an added spark of understanding. Smiling, the Master said, 'Fill your nursery with seeds. Make the effort. Take the time it takes, however long that is. Growth does occur. Allow life to take its course'. The Master smiled. The young man smiled back.

30
Concentrate on the Sun

We are in fog, looking for sun.
Our guides say to use the compasses just so:
'Head to the sun – always.'

Just so, we affirm, and
Keep going.
We keep going, knowing – inevitably,
We will find the sun.

Sunlight endures,
Fog dissolves,
Revealing itself to us and
Us to ourselves –
Now alight.

Compared to Light, life is fog,
A fog we know
For what it is,
Though memory holds nothing
To compare it to the Light.

Just so, in meditation too, we can act
To make the Light our own.

We keep meditating and meditating.
The fog begins to break – at times.

We keep meditating and meditating.
The fog is left behind – occasionally to return.

We keep meditating and meditating.
The fog dissolves – gone forever.

Revealed in the Light,
Revealing our Selves to ourselves,
Real Life begins in dazzling display –
Unfolding Eternity.

31
Make It as Easy as Possible

'In the modern world we expect virtually everything to turn out the way we plan it.' The Master was talking to several people in their early twenties. They had been complaining mightily about his repeated assertion that they needed to keep meditating, if they wanted results. They thought he was old fashioned and he decided to respond as if they were right. 'We are now accustomed to our technology guaranteeing most outcomes. Think of several examples: Transport can usually get through, no matter the conditions; communications are maintained under almost all circumstances; even some of our bodies parts can be replaced when they wear out. We have the technologies to do all of these things and more.' Some of his listeners stirred restlessly as he continued.

'Even fifty years ago, life was far less certain and predictable, while over a hundred years ago, it was very unpredictable. When people set out on a journey, they did not assume that they would arrive. They appreciated that many events might prevent this.

Communication was much slower and also less reliable. International letters would take months or years to arrive, and this was expected. Health was a prized possession, something that was accepted with a sense of gratitude rather than as a right. Many, perhaps most, forms of ill-health were much more of a risk, much more likely to be fatal. Even illnesses, such as colds and flu were very serious and could easily end in death.'

The what-is-the-point-of-all-this looks were on almost every face by this time. The Master introduced a soothing tone to his voice, amused by their get-to-the-point impatience. 'There was an accepted sense, during these times, that people had to do things for themselves to get the results they wanted. Also, because of the risks, "nothing" was guaranteed. The best anyone could do on any task was to do as much as possible to get the results and hope everything else would fall into place. These days, things are very different. Many people won't accepted the same kind of effort as necessary any more. In the West, we look for easy, guaranteed ways of doing things, or, if possible, ways around having to do anything very much at all.

'Naturally, the same pattern is evident in the way some of you approach your meditation. You want guaranteed results with as little effort from you as possible. You have come to expect this sort of thing. However, meditation is still relatively free of technology; in this area technology cannot yet guarantee outcomes.' The

Master looked around, seeing dawning awareness on their faces about where he was going with all this. 'So it is up to you. Only your own efforts will guarantee the results. No one and nothing else can do it for you. It is you who needs to put in the time. Without "machinery", if you want Awakening, you need to do the learning, to develop the skills and the experience that will enable you to manage your consciousness as required.

'I realise that some of you may be unwilling to do what is necessary. Actually, this has been true throughout history. Not everyone wants Awakening enough to put in the necessary effort. However, for committed ones, there are ways of making it as easy as possible – a "type of technology". I have already taught you some of this. First, associate with realised people as much as possible. Their realisation directly stimulates yours. Second, join with others in meditation as much as possible, for what we share intensifies. Third, make it fun, so you enjoy yourself and want to do it. Last and most importantly, meditate repeatedly.'

32

Guru Glamour

*(For the word 'Guru' you can read 'Master',
'Spirit', 'God' – or anything that represents the
Infinite in your life.)*

The glamour of it all: 'Oh to be important and accomplished and Awakened like the Guru. And, if not important and accomplished and Awakened like the Guru, then to be thought important and accomplished and at least a little Awakened, by the Guru. And, if not actually thought important and accomplished and at least a little Awakened by the Guru, then at least to imagine that we have importance and accomplishment and Awakening in the eyes of the Guru. And, if not actually to have any imagined importance, accomplishment and a little Awakening like the Guru's, in the eyes if the Guru, then at least to have the solace of making up whatever seems to make us important, accomplished and a little Awakened to the Guru and spread this abroad and convince as many others as possible to think us important, accomplished and a little Awakened by the Guru. Oh smile on, my Beloved Guru, that I may turn you into an effigy of my heart's desire, whatever your Reality.'

Many people are so hungry for recognition, so craving for Awakening, and so confused about how to proceed, that they notice even the smallest events and build them into something big. Picking through the trivia of each encounter, hoped-for crumbs can appear where they are not. The most insignificant gesture, look, act – anything – can be built into something it is not, was never intended to be, something innocent of Transcendent Significance. Sometimes a wave of the hand is simply to move a fly to another part of the room. Sometimes a look is casual and passing, not laden with significance, not recognition of some deep change that just took place a moment before, or a precognitive awareness of something that occurred a moment afterwards. The truth is that we need to give up all of this. The value is that as the glamour fades, often accompanied by our deep regret as we accept reality, our Realisation grows.

And what of all those people who parade around talking about how the Guru did this, and the Guru did that, and the Guru guided me to do this and that? What of their own real capacities – to discriminate, to make decisions, to act? Is the Guru responsible for them looking both ways when they cross the road so that they avoid accidents? Was it actually the Guru that prevented them from walking in front of the car that they saw heading in their direction? Does the Guru put the postage stamps on the letters they send?

We look at the Guru and see the True Light of True Awakening, hear its Wondrous Sounds, feel the immediate stirring of Awakening in the flesh-based consciousness of every cell in our bodies, breathe and drink in the Sweet Fragrance of the Ultimate expressed in the Guru's human form. Attracted naturally to the Beauty, wanting It, hungering for It to take us over and transmute us, it is temptingly easy to imagine events. The glamourous glitter of reflected light, the strident sound of unconvincing voices, the empty tension of imagined hopes held high, the artificial taste and fragrance of manufactured beauty, is as nothing compared to the Reality of Real Beauty. Realising the Reality of our actual states, unembellished by hope's premature distortion, is the fastest path to your own Reality, to your own Guru-hood.

33

Realise in Every Moment

'Everything we need and have in life is in the present moment. If we miss each moment, then we miss Life.' The Master paused to look around the room, deliberately taking in each person. 'Our lives generally are the sum of all our present moments and, very importantly, our general styles set up momentum in everything we do. We need to pay attention to this, lest the momentum in our living makes difficult, or completely prevents us from doing what we need to do to Realise the Awakening we crave.

'Do you walk along the street, or a corridor and notice where you are? When you pick up the telephone, do you notice what you are doing? Are you aware as you do things – peeling the vegetables, writing a letter, studying for exams, washing the floor, driving the car? Do you notice the children when they talk to you, and your friends, your husband, wife or partner? Do you always see where you are, hear the sounds, notice the air? Do flowers and plants still have texture and fragrance for you? Do you taste the food you are eating any more? Or is your momentum carrying you away from all of this, away from your only access way to Life?

'Many people inadvertently trap themselves by confusing busyness with "productivity". Just because they're doing something, they think they're doing something effective to reach their goals. Another trap is to allow our meditation practice to revert to a previous style, a style that, when we started meditating, we wanted to change? Take a moment to think if this is true for you. Think about your life. Are you heading for Full Realisation? Or are you reverting to old patterns again?'

The Master was talking to a mixed group and had their complete attention. Some were students, who 'had become' too busy with study to take the time to meditate. Others were business people, some of whom used to meditate regularly, who had for a long time been trying to squeeze their practice into a few snatched minutes a day. Home makers, teachers, professional people, office and factory workers, sat side by side, all were allowing their daily activities to drive their lives. Too busy to notice what they were doing in each moment, all of them were diminishing the Life they could experience directly in their lives.

'So practise awareness and meditate diligently. Your life depends on it, for, as I said before, the Life in your life comes to you in the noticing of every moment. Through meditating, you deepen your connection to and the flow of the Life that animates you. And it needs to be real meditation, not a ritualistic or token practice. So much – infinitely more than you currently imagine – will open up for you, as you do these two things.'

34
Getting Clear of the Fog

It was a dreary winter's day outside. Everyone sat near a fire that was giving golden warmth to the Master's living room. Outwardly appearing to meditate, the Master was enjoying the sharp contrast between the crackling of the burning wood and the peaceful atmosphere. After a while, he looked outside at the darkening sky above the thickening ground fog that heralded evening.

'Soon you won't be able to see your hand in front of your face out there', he observed. 'It reminds me of a time I was driving around the city years ago in a very thick fog. It was night and all we could see was the reflection of our own car lights off the fog in front of us. Many people just stopped and gave up trying to progress, choosing to accept the situation and wait for the fog to lift enough to see even a little before trying to go further. Some slept in their cars overnight. Others pressed on very slowly, using glimpses of the curb, white lines on the road, or other barely visible features to guide them. Some drivers were able to navigate enough by using the extra they could see in the lights of other cars in front of them. Still others, hoping that the driver immediately ahead knew where he or she was going, followed the tail lights.

'It took a long time to get home that night, but presumably everyone did eventually, although not without incident for some. One funny story was recounted in the papers the next day of a driver, who, having followed the car ahead for quite some time, noticed it stop and someone get out of the driver's door. Thinking there was a problem, he got out too and went forward to investigate, to be met half way by the other driver coming back to him. "What are you doing?" the lead driver challenged. "I've been following you", the second driver replied. "Well mate, you've ended up in my driveway; is that where you wanted to be?" They both laughed, enjoying the comedy of the situation.'

'That whole experience is similar to what it's like during the "foggy" times of meditation.' He emphasised the 'foggy' with mild irony. 'You know, the times: When you don't know what's going on, you've lost your bearings, you can't see a thing and you seem so stuck that you can't go forward or backwards with any certainty.' 'That sounds like most of my life to me', one of the clowns in the group exclaimed. Everyone laughed with the mirth of shared understanding.

'Well, interestingly, that story shows everyone what to do, to get clear of a meditative fog', the Master went on. 'Notice a few things. First, you knew where you were going when you set out. The fog doesn't change your destination. Second, remember that the fog will lift, no matter how thick it is, so even if you need to wait for a long time, all you have to do is wait, if necessary, and you can progress again. Third, you may be able to make careful progress by paying attention to the available signs that show where you are. Fourth, your fellow meditators may be of some help, in that their progress can light the way for you to some extent, or show you aspects of the road that you might otherwise have missed. But, fifth, if you follow someone blindly, you need to be prepared for the possibility of ending up in someone else's back yard, rather than where you intended to go.'

35
Sun of Life, Clouds of Complaint

'Life bathes us in its warmth, lights our way and shows us the path to tread to our own completion. So beautifully intense, so wondrous, so gloriously alive that we cannot possibly forever hold out against it, Life will express itself through us, one way or another. Life is expressing itself through us, right now.' Those with 'the sight', could see Resplendent Light streaming from the Master as he spoke. He was a living exemplar of what he said. Those who could not 'see' were, nevertheless, aware of his animation, his body's celebration every time he said "Life", the bubbling joy in his voice that added flavour to every word. 'Life is for Living, Actual Living', he finished with a flourish.

Some, caught up in his enthusiasm, had begun to smile. Others, still holding themselves in the complaints he had interrupted, were looking sulky and resistant. The try-and-make-me-enjoy-myself looks on their faces needed no interpreter.

'From the Sun's point of view, everything and everyone gets the Life available. It shines equally on all. From the recipient's point of view, this may not seem true, for it is their demeanour in life, their attitudes, their availability, that determine how much Sun they think they have shining on them. From the Sun's point of view, these people are like little patches of cloud, cloud that blocks more or less well the penetration of the Life that the Sun offers at every moment.' Still no sign of change from some people present, although more had begun to allow themselves to soften and open to the Master's enthusiasm. The 'professionals' were still not prepared to let go, however. Clouds at the ready, they were marching forth into battle, their slogan, 'Try to make me happy, if you dare!'

'I don't want this. I don't want that. This is wrong. That's wrong.' As the Master counted these statements out of his mouth on his fingers, he mimicked the looks, the posture and the tones of someone who was working at suffering, 'catastrophising', 'awfuling', or exaggerating dejection. He was so good at it that almost everyone was laughing loudly as he finished. 'We should give an award to the ones with the most complaints, the ones who can see most fault in the things and people around them. After all, it takes real talent to find darkness in the midst of such profound Light and Life.' He laughed enthusiastically as he spoke, poking and nudging a few of the 'professionals' close to him. Others were falling about themselves with laughter as they recognised the humour and the poignant futility of what they had been doing.

'Just remember everyone, the Sun is shining. Life is in every moment and is always with us in its full glory. All you need to do is make yourself available to it. Surrounding yourself in a cloud of complaints only blocks your view. It does not block Life. So why do it? Commit to Life. Forget your complaints. Forget the injustices you have collected, the hurts, the letdowns. Let the warm Light of Life evaporate your personal cloud. It will do it if you practise awareness of the Sun in your life, but not if you don't. It's up to you. All you need to do is to take responsibility for yourself and to stop imagining and acting as if your life is someone else's responsibility.' Finally, they all got the point.

37
Clearing the Pond

Imagine yourself as a muddy, or stagnant pond. You contain water. You also contain suspended material, rotting vegetation and mud. Your bottom is covered in the accumulated slime of years. While not a pretty picture, most of us are in a similar state when we first start to meditate. The years of holding onto our experiences, of inhibiting the free expression of our aliveness, of blocking our awareness of all that we have been taught is unacceptable, have their effects. The years of living like this cut us off more and more from the source of Life within us, turning us into pale shadows of our possible Glory. We become clogged up, sometimes stagnant, we become dull and decreasingly Life-filled.

To engage in Awakening activities helps to reverse the effects of our previous ways of living. We start to flow, to express, to celebrate, to cultivate awareness. We start to flood with Life and to live the Life flooding through us. The results are stimulating for almost everyone, and rewarding, provided we persist. Following a definite progression, the process of engaging in these activities is like clearing the muddy pond.

Imagine, now, that crystal clear water is pouring into you, the muddy, stagnant pond that you were imagining yourself to be. In the beginning, the water gradually fills the pond until it is overflowing, just as meditating on Life Energy fills you to overflowing. If this process disturbs the surface, an unpleasant smell may be released, as old material, long held suspended, begins to move. And once the pond is overflowing, the outflowing water generally carries away the material that is nearest the outlet. Moreover, looking at the outflow, you will be able to see that much of what was previously caught is suspended in the water, which will look anything but crystal clear.

When beginning to meditate, our experiences can be similar, for as our energetic flow begins and progressively increases, we start to overflow, too. What is carried out are the feelings, thoughts, memories, desires, hopes, impulses, physical experiences and old attitudes that became caught in our systems as we lived our lives. Because this is not always a pleasant process, we may occasionally wonder why we ever wanted to begin to meditate, particularly if we hoped, or were told that it would make our lives easier. Fortunately, however, people often also experience a sense of the underlying cleansing.

Persistence pays off, too. As with the pond, provided we continue to pour the crystal clear waters of our Meditative Energy into ourselves, we will eventually clear completely. And, just Like the outflow of the pond, our 'outflowing experiences' become increasingly clear too. By persisting, we discover that everything keeps changing provided we continue our meditative practices. Whatever the contents of our experience, we learn that the Clarity we want is inevitable. We only need to keep flooding ourselves with the Clarity that comes from every moment of meditation in order that we, like the pond, will become completely Clear.

To hasten the process, we can engage in various other activities, too. Just as we used to stir up the mud deliberately, when playing with water as children, we can do specialised exercises, such as yoga, tai chi, Tibetan exercises, or dynamic movement to help us release our histories more easily and comfortably. Also, we can spend time with people who are more enlivened than ourselves, with the purpose of intensifying the flooding of Life into our own systems. This is like increasing the flow of water into the pond as a means of accelerating the cleansing process.

It always helps through these times to remember: 'The pond will clear. You will Awaken. Just stick at it.'

38
Love Produces Union; Anger, Division

A man and a woman had been arguing loudly when the Master came into the room. Both were red in the face from their exertions, their fists were clenched, their eyes glassy and bulging. They were disconcerted by the Master's appearance, like people suddenly stopped in the middle of a running race. Taking in the scene and the causes at a glance, he walked away towards a nearby window seat and sat down. The couple looked after him, wondering what he was going to do.

'Come here, you two', he said firmly. His tone brooked no dissent and they did what he said quickly, demure with him, though still scowling at each other. He began to speak, 'I have something for you to do with each other ...', but was rudely interrupted as they both began shouting, putting their own cases, as if he was to be their judge. 'Be quiet!' he yelled above their din. Silenced by his tone, they looked at him in surprise, never having heard him speak like this before. 'This is not the way. Now, listen to me and do what I tell you.'

'Sit opposite each other.' They did what he instructed.
'Now, hold hands and look at each other, in the eyes
preferably. If you don't think you can manage the eyes
just yet, at least see who is sitting in front of you. Also,
notice what you are sitting on, notice your contact with
what is underneath you.' Obviously a little more
relaxed, although each was still holding out against the
other, the man and woman did what he said. He let
them do this for a few minutes, interrupting them
twice, when they started to talk to continue their argument. As time passed, however, they became much
more settled.

Eventually, the Master said, 'Now keep doing what you
are doing, and each of you notice your heart. Feel it
inside your chest, look at it there – internally that is.
Listen to it, taste or smell it, or talk about it to yourself.
Just keep it in your awareness'. He paused for a few minutes more to allow them enough time to get used to doing
this. Then he went on, giving them one step at a time:
'Now feel the warmth, see the soft light, hear the mellow-
ness, and taste and smell the sweetness and fragrance of
the love that is there in your experience. All you need to
do to release this love is to notice your heart'. Following
his instructions, the two of them quickly began to mel-
low, their faces becoming soft and rounded, the glaring of
their eyes melting quickly into yielding, receptivity and
mutually aware pools of openness.

After a few more minutes, the Master said, 'Now repeat
the Mantra "I AM Love" and keep noticing the love in

your hearts as you do. Also, keep looking at each other'. They did as instructed and quickly melted into a warm, tender hug, the argument now apparently behind them.

'The cause of your argument doesn't matter to me', the Master said after a while. 'At times, couples need to "discuss" things – preferably the facts – to sort them out. It's important that they do. Always remember as you do, however, that love produces union and anger produces division. If you would have union, immerse yourselves in love. If you would have division, culti-vate anger.

'Love is the more powerful of the two feelings, because union is the more natural state. So love will dissolve anger, provided we stay aware of what we love and care about when we feel angry. The trick is to express our-selves in terms of what we love and care about, what we want, rather than what we don't want. Our anger is then drawn into and dissolves in the process of find-ing practical solutions to our disputes. What is very important in this is that by acting in this way, we can draw ourselves together in our disagreements.'

39

Experience

A Doorway from Less to More

'I was meditating the other day and was struck again by
the apparent contradictions we find along the way to
Enlightenment. So much of what we need to learn is to
do with balancing opposites, finding common ground,
travelling the middle way, combining the incompatible,
with finding possibilities in impossibilities. The nature
of the human experience seems to compel us to do this.'
The Master was talking to a large group of people who
had come to meditate with him.

'We would be One with All That Is, yet we are in a
seemingly divided, fragmented state. We would be saturated in the Divine, by all that lies out of normal experience in the Beyond, while seemingly we remain locked
into normal experience so tightly that escape seems
impossible. Yet, as we persist, the opposites do dissolve
into union, incompatibilities do turn out to be illusions
that hide the basic Oneness in all things, impossibilities
are revealed as insubstantial clouds that obscure options
that are so profound that everything becomes possible.

'The Ultimate is the centre of all, the basis of Life Itself, the core from which everything arises, the Being in all that exists, the Light of Life – Infinite and eternal, so vast that no one still centered in their worldliness can conceive or contain it. The physical frame that is the basis of much of our lives simply cannot in its beginning form accommodate the Infinity that the Ultimate is. Yet that is precisely what we need it to do for us to become Fully Awakened. We need to learn to accommodate, to integrate with, to become a channel for the Ultimate.

'And how do we do this?

'We do it by repeatedly going into our bodies, into our worldly experiences. We do it by learning to become so saturated in, so completely aligned and at one with our bodily and body-based experiences that we live them completely. To succeed, we need to do this with on-going awareness, a process that takes patient practice.

'In the beginning, for many people, this is like going into a cave, into what seems like darkness there. And we need to let go of the apparent light of the world to go "in". We turn our backs, as it were, on the "outside" phenomena and turn "inwards". During the process, we learn to face the "inner" phenomena. And in so doing, we discover progressively the many Wonders within ourselves; for example, that the darkness we entered with such trepidation disappears instantly when exposed to even just a spark of Real Light, that even a hint of Divine Love dissolves disunity and that Deep Harmony and Divine Silence settle all discordance.

'The wonders we discover are the Light, Love, Harmony and Silence of Life. And as we persist, our perception of Life becomes purer; we become clearer, more alive and alight, more resoundingly melodious or quietly tranquil, more fragrant, sweet and blissful. We know that progress is sure – eventually – although in the beginning it may seem anything but sure. And as this wondrous unfolding occurs, tentatively at first, it seems that we are coming out of the cave of our worldliness into the Light and Love of the Ultimate. And then we emerge.

'Once there, once in the Light, Love and Harmony, we know things differently. We can fathom the apparent contradictions in our experience. While it seemed that we were losing the light by "going into" experience, we were gaining the Light of Life. While it seemed that we were going into the confining cave of worldliness, we were discovering that this cave was our only avenue to release us from our confinement into the vast dimensions of Ultimate Experience. So instead of the cave leading us to less, as it seemed when we entered, it became our doorway through "less" to vastly more than we could ever imagine.

'Far from being a small spark lost in blackness, we discover Life in its Transcendent, Brilliant, Harmonious and Vibrant Vastness, a Vastness in the midst of which our worldliness is a "nothing doorway" into Everything.'

40
Enlightened Tripping

Travelling these days is routine. Once, however, it was a much more haphazard affair. We could not guarantee our time of arrival, nor, under many circumstances, that we would arrive at all. Travelling often used to involve great effort, too. Technology has, however, changed much of this.

We now expect to arrive under virtually all circumstances and we expect to arrive more or less on time. Some people even consider suing for damages, if they do not arrive as expected. Another dimension of recent technological developments is that we no longer need to put much personal effort into the process of travelling. We climb aboard the vehicle that will carry us, and the machinery and those responsible for running it do all of the work.

A related consequence of these change is that journeys are now strongly associated with entertainment, rather than effort. We look for ways of filling in the time the journey takes, not for how we can contribute to arriving safely and in good order. Responsibility is in the hands of the travel staff. We are genuine passengers, no longer the crew in any sense.

Many people try and meditate in the same way. They approach the process like passengers, not as crew members. They do not realise that their progress (the travelling) depends on their own efforts. They want the results (like getting to the destination) guaranteed, but they avoid or are ignorant of the necessity to apply themselves to the task of travelling (like doing the walking, driving, flying, climbing). They have lost, or have never had, the connection between their own efforts and the progress they make.

Meditation is much more like the old ways of travelling. The outcome is assured only if we put in the effort to reach the destination. We are our own crew members. We cannot catch someone else's bus or plane to Enlightenment. While we might find entertainment in our progress at times, the progress we make with meditation comes from our own efforts. And we only get to the end of the journey, if we do what is required.

Also, we are in charge of our own travel arrangements. Others can contribute, of course. However, those who have made the trip before may only help as travel guides, or companions, or as consultant mechanics on how to keep the vehicle in good shape as we travel. The rest is up to us.

41
Turn From 'Replica Living' to Real Life

The world seems to surround us with its size and power. We can seem so puny in relation to it. The world seems capable of sweeping us aside in the blink of an eye. Vulnerability stares us in the face.

At the same time, we can see such beauty in this world, such creativity and life. So much is so vibrant, so full of its own harmony, so filled with the fragrance and sweetness of Life itself. Children know this as they play from moment to moment, held in the trance of timelessness, perceiving in this heavenly thrall the wonder of Creation in all its Glory. They have not yet learnt to see as they will be taught to see, to hear as they will be taught to hear, to feel the touch as they are taught to feel it, to taste or smell as they will be taught to taste and smell.

'Oh no', said with a laugh, 'that's just a raven with lustrous black feathers swooping in to land, not a mighty

ball of flying energy blown by the wind and flowing
into the sun's glow beside us here'. Or, 'What do you
mean, you got the answer because the colour was right?
You can't do arithmetic that way, you little cheat'. Or,
'Daddy/Mummy listen to that', to which we reply, 'Oh
that's a so and so', instead of just listening and with a
long, rapturous sigh, saying, 'Aaah', and again, 'Aaah,
yes'.

Very early we learn to stop hearing, seeing, touching,
tasting and smelling the original. We settle for reflec-
tions, shadows, replicas – and filtered, distorted replicas
at that. And eventually we don't even know what we
have lost any more. All we know is that we have lost
something, because an unfathomable, empty presence
inside us echoes a past, pure, real impact that still
reaches us down through the years.

True seeing is completely different from trained seeing.
The same applies to true hearing, touching, tasting and
smelling. And how do we know this, if we have lost
perception of the original? We know because the original is still in the replica. As hard as we may try, we
cannot succeed in removing the original. Fortunately
for us, it is the very substance that we pour into the
mould of our learnt living. Its presence always reminds
us of what we are missing. Its presence still stirs the
living parts of us that still always perceive the truth of
life, even after we have learnt through long years not to
notice it.

The path to Life is obvious in this: Quest and find the
original; only settle for what is actually stimulating
you, the Source of what you think you know; don't settle for less. Turn and look at the sun. Use its reflection to remind you of its Origin and turn again in
celebration to find that Origin. Find the Source of
sound in what you hear, rather than easily accepting
the remnants that reach you through your training
dulled ears. Find the Infinity of Bliss and Joy, of Love
and Life that you feel as a hint in your current life's
highs. Taste and smell the Sweet Nectar and Fragrance
of the Origin. Only settle for that.

Embrace Life fully. Realise that your life is a replica of
Life. And within your life, turn about to face Your
Source. Allow Reality to begin to seep into you again,
and once seeping, to begin to flow, and then to cascade,
and, finally, to inundate you completely. Just give It
the chance. You will Live.

42

To Persist Or Not to Persist

'I feel I'm drifting away from so much that used to be so important to me.' The statement was filled with yearning, with challenge, with uncertainty, and with a tugging inertia that bordered on indolence. The Master also heard hope for release and a desire to be motivated to return to the old ways. Remembering his own crisis, he said, 'Your life is yours to live as you wish, or as you decide'. Looking crestfallen and relieved at the same time, the speaker said, 'Oh, I thought you'd try to make me keep going'. The Master paused meditatively, 'I wouldn't do that; you are at a cross-road in your life and it's your choice which way you go. With your experience, you know where each route takes you. Now it's up to you. Only in the beginning was it help-ful for me to urge you to continue. At that stage, you had no real idea of the benefits of doing so'.

The two of them sat on in silence. 'I remember the choice well and I've seen others have to face it, too. After years of dedication, of striving for "success", we get to a point where something "inside" switches. We wonder if it's worth it: The meditating every day, the deliberate doing of things we would often rather not do, and the hopes for rewards, for satisfaction – for Enlightenment. Is it worth it? What would it matter if I just settled back now? Why not just settle for what I feel I am, for what I've got? Besides, there are so many other things that I'd like to do, so many things I see my friends and colleagues doing with the extra time they have because they don't meditate.'

It was obvious that the Master had hit the spot. 'Yes, yes, yes – I often feel as if I can't be bothered any more', a pause and a flicker of sheepishness crosses his face, 'and I blame you at times. You said we would all get there, that it was beautiful, that it was worth any effort, that all we had to do was to stick to it'. Then with a defiant glint in his eye, 'Well I've done all that and I'm still not there. I don't think I want to bother any more'.

Completely at ease, the Master said, 'I'm glad. Your not wanting to bother will make you face yourself more deeply than every before. Many people begin meditating for reasons that will not carry them through to Enlightenment. Some do it to find a mummy or daddy who loves them, some to be better than others, some to make their pain go away, some to fill inner gaps, some to develop powers that make them special – many different reasons. All of them, almost without exception, put the power of their practice outside themselves. But when it comes down to it, the only reasons that will endure are the ones that arise from deep within us, reasons that flow out of our need to Fulfil ourselves by coming back Home "inside". The only motivation that works completely is the desire for Oneness with the Ultimate from which we arose in the first place. The power of this motivation is Infinite and "inside".

'The way I see it, your crisis is about growing up as a meditator. Are you going to take responsibility for yourself now? Will you do what is required, or will you decide the goal isn't worth it? Given what you know from your own experience now, are you willing to decide to forego what could be around the corner, or many years away? These are some of your choices. Your life from here on will show your answers.'

The Master paused, then said with a glint in his eye, 'I still think it's worth continuing'.

43

Knowing and Learning Freely

A woman excitedly told the Master about something she had learnt in a workshop on the previous weekend. It had been a completely new revelation to her. 'I was so pleased, because it helped me put all sorts of things together that I have been struggling with for years.' 'How often I've heard that', the Master said, leaning back and surveying the young woman sitting in front of him.

Puzzled by his comment, she asked, 'What do you mean, you've heard it often?' 'Well', he began, 'I mean that I am always intrigued and excited by what people do to learn new things. You have just come to me very excited about something that will make a very big difference in your life – something that, from your point of view, is completely new. Is that right?' She nodded vigorously. 'What intrigues me is that I have been teaching you that lesson for many years now.' He fell silent, waiting.

She looked pensive for quite some time, then she suddenly brightened. 'Oh I see what you mean. Yes – I

was presenting what I said as if no one else had contributed to my learning, when, in fact, you and quite a
few others have contributed lots.' 'Mmm, that's part of
it', the Master said to encourage her to keep thinking
and talking. 'Yes, what I was feeling was that I had to
pretend you had not played a part in my learning, as if
I would lose something if I acknowledged your contribution, or anyone else's for that matter.' 'That's what I
observed', the Master said. 'Many people do this.'

'The trouble with doing it, however, is that we have to
keep cutting off from our previous sources of learning
so that we have a sense of progress. We progress at the
expense of the past, not with the aid of the past. Do
you understand what I mean by this?' Another reflec-
tive silence followed. 'I think I do', she finally said. 'I
always felt that I had to fight my parents so they would
take notice of what I thought was important and right.
I got the impression that they didn't value what I said.
So I ended up rejecting their points of view. I felt I
couldn't learn for myself, unless I rejected them. Now
I realise that I was doing something similar with you –
and that I've done it with most of the important people
in my life.'

'What you have realised is very significant, but there is
more to it than you currently understand.' She looked
at him attentively. 'With your position, you can't be
fully open to learning from others, because your are
always likely to feel suspicious of them. Also, you will
need to move on from them eventually so you feel that

you know what you have learnt. And you are unlikely to understand that everyone has knowledge, or that two people can know the same thing at the same time without an emotional cost to either.' He paused until she nodded for him to go on. ' But most important of all, this approach keeps people cut off from fully accepting their own Divinity. They have to hold themselves back, because they sense that one day they will have to prove that they know better than God. The only way they can do this is by separating themselves from their Sources. Of course, this is the opposite of what is needed for Awakening.'

She showed the sudden shock of understanding the enormity of her previous position. It was quickly followed by relief. Then she smiled and warmly reached out. As they hugged he said into her ear, 'Practise honouring your origins by becoming one with them'.

44
It All Just Happens Now?

To hear what many people say these days, they imply that they and we don't do anything in life. We are the hapless victims of happenstance, that is, circumstances. 'Everything' just happens. Accidents happen, pregnancy happens, drug taking happens, physical assaults happen. No one is responsible, it seems, unless, of course, the outcomes are desirable and could bring praise.

These people say, for example, 'When it happened', not 'When I did it'. The verbal clues are clear. First, people use 'it' instead of words like 'I', 'he', 'she', 'we', 'they', or 'you'. Second, they use 'happens', 'happened', 'will happen', or 'happening'.

Very significantly, this kind of thing strengthens 'victim consciousness'. When acting in this kind of way we rarely experience ourselves doing things with our own power. Instead, we act as if the actions we take are somehow independent of our volition: 'I didn't do it', 'I didn't mean to do it', 'I couldn't help it'. All of this seems very like children trying to slide out of trouble.

Acting as if life is happening is both disempowering for us and involves shifts of responsibility for what we have done. However, no matter what we pretend, if I have done something, I did it; if you have done something, you did it; if we have done something together, we did it; and if they have done something, they did it. And, whomever did the something is responsible for having done it.

So experiment right now as you read, stand up, raise your hands, drop your hands to your sides, say 'Yes', say 'No'. Now sit down again and think about what you have just done. You were responsible for each act, even for not following the suggested instructions, if that is what you did.

In summary, whatever we do, we are responsible.

Understanding this is very important when we seek Enlightenment. Our Spiritual Awakening depends on it. Enlightenment doesn't just happen to anyone. It requires action, effort, persistence, and commitment on each of our parts. Anything we each need to do, is something that we each need to do. Only we can do it, too, no one else.

Enlightenment is a big thing to achieve, since it is to do with 'Ultimate States', and to do what is required involves embracing the Full Power each of us has. Exercising the capacity to decide what to do and then doing it is fundamental in this. So people who act as if what they do arises without their control will miss the

Power, because they are diminishing their power by avoiding their responsibility for their actions. The simple truth is that we only expand in Light and Life as we claim both our personal power and our responsibilities for what we do and who we are.

So, how can we do this? A very simple approach is to affirm 'I Am responsible' repeatedly. More specifically, we can affirm, 'I Am responsible' whatever we observe about ourselves and whatever we observe in the world around us. Both are very empowering practices – and responsible.

45

Who Can Ever Even Dream What Is Ahead?

Several new arrivals had turned up to meditation. One was there out of curiosity; another because he was hurting and wanting to feel better; the next because she was ill and looking for something to help. The last, another young woman, was there for Enlightenment. Perhaps it was unusual to have them all there on one night, but it was the usual spread of reasons, seen thousands of times.

They were there to find out about meditation and what it could offer them. The first explanation they heard might have a crucial effect on them, so it would be important to link in with what they wanted, what they understood and what they could reasonably expect to get.

The Master sat meditating on what he would say. So much was possible for each of them and would remain so, even if they didn't understand this on their first night. Nevertheless, what he would say was important. In his experience, thousands upon thousands had proved what was possible by meditating and getting wonderful results. He knew, too, that millions of others had proved this as well. And what results they had been! Many had got what they had wanted, and many others, much, much more. Some had recovered their health, others had learnt to cope with their lives and were now happy. Some had experienced a touch of Enlightenment, even Enlightenment itself.

As he sat meditating, the right words started to form, pressing from deep inside him for expression. When they finally reached his mouth, he began, 'If you start today and you keep doing what I suggest, I guarantee that you will get the results you want, probably far more. This is a big thing to promise and I do promise it. What I can't guarantee, however, is how long it will take you to get it, or if you will have the tenacity to keep going for as long as it will take you. I hope that you do. As you persist, you will need to do two things: Repeat the Mantra I will give you tonight as often as you can until it reveals itself in your Being, and master some other practical things I can teach you to make your life easy and balanced'. Then he said something special to each person in turn that was designed to awaken them uniquely.

As usual, he was met variously with hope, vague comprehension, confusion – and from them all, virtually no understanding of what was possible. They all wanted to understand; they were not resisting. They could not, however, do the impossible – just yet. They all needed at least to glimpse the brilliance, to feel briefly the love, or to have even a moment of the deep, sweet, joyous silence, so they could discover what lies within us all. In that instant, they would know how the transformations they were questing would come to them. They would have a direct experience that could keep them going for life, if necessary, that would also help them expand those moments into hours, days, months and years. They would experience Life in all its wonder, wonder that is revealed to everyone through persisting on the path to Enlightenment. Until that moment of revelation, they, like all of us who have passed the same way, would just need to practise the suggestions. If they did, success would be theirs.

'Who can even dream of what lies ahead?' mused the Master, as he bent towards the first in order to transmit the Mantra. 'The Beauty, the Love, the Fulfilment of what we can have in our day-to-day lives seems to be way beyond comprehension. Ah, though, when it comes directly, everything is possible.'

46
Life Rattles Our Cages to Show They Aren't There

Most people live as if they are in a cage, as if they are confined and unable to act freely. Mostly they don't realise they are doing this. Without the awareness of how free they could be, they don't realise they are confining themselves. They are living automatically, for example, rather than saying or doing things that they are free to say and do. They don't realise that the capacity to complete things, the understanding and wisdom that come with Awakening, the Love that is inherent in everything, is actually available to them – right now.

The deep, abiding reality is that none of us is actually caged. We are free to decide whatever we decide, and to do whatever we choose. We are free to experience the full richness of life. We are free to know Awakening. And nothing can stop us, except ourselves. Any apparent difficulties arise only because we have confined ourselves to our imaginary cages, not because these are a basic part of us or the world in which we live.

Fortunately for us, in every moment of our lives, 'reality' calls us to open up to our true freedoms. We participate in this opening process by helping to create all of the events in our lives. These face us every day with the option either of using our real freedom, or of committing ourselves yet again to the cages with which we have surrounded ourselves in our imaginations. The way this works is through challenge. As we, for example, contemplate saying things we normally would not say, doing things we normally would not do, or even just wanting to do these things, the bars start to rattle. And as they rattle, we become aware that they are there.

People's responses to the rattling bars vary. First, some people just move away from the bars so they stop disturbing them, or so they can no longer hear them, perhaps by giving up and settling for a lot less than they could. Second, they might try to stop them rattling, perhaps by convincing themselves that they really are confined and that they should strengthen what is limiting them. Third, they might try to open the door or to break out through the bars, perhaps by struggling to find new capacities that they can use to open up their lives. Notice, however, that all of these options involve accepting that their cages are real. Therefore, all of these options strengthen their illusion.

The most powerful way to proceed is to act on the assumption that we are already free. Nothing contains us. So when, for example, we think, 'Oh, I couldn't do that', we can think instead, 'Ah yes, I can do that'. If we conceive of ourselves as free, then we can much more easily act accordingly, than if we don't. By doing this we claim what is fundamentally true and build on that truth. Then, just like shadows exposed to light, every time we act according to this truth, our cages evaporate. They turn out to have no substance of their own.

The freedom we have craved is revealed to have been always ours. Then we discover that everything is easier and has always been that way.

47
Put on a Likeness of God

All is One in God. God is Infinite and Eternal. God is
Love, Joy, Light, Sweetness. God is Truth. And these
are not just theoretical statements. They are enduring
realities, realities that we can each experience increasingly with the expansion of Awakening. God is also in
and through everything. God is the Very Stuff from
which everything arises.

How, then, if we are made 'in the image and likeness of
God', as we are told, are our lives so contracted, difficult, unhappy and unfulfilled? The simple answer is
that we live as if we are not at one with God and so
block ourselves from experiencing what this Oneness
is. We have been trained to believe that we are puny
creatures. We have learnt to avoid, deny, contain, control and constrict, to plough our spontaneity under the
sods of other people's expectations, to act in ways that
disconnect us from our souls. We can end up almost
completely cut off, strangled or blocked from the flow
of Life that is God in our lives.

Much of the process of Awakening involves reclaiming
our Godhood. Somehow we need to open up to God

117

again and embrace all that God is – a seemingly big task. Yet if we understand three basic realities, we can realise that it is not nearly so big. First, we are made of God-stuff, so every aspect of ourselves knows what God is like, even if this knowledge is 'deeply buried'. Second, God flows through every aspect of us as Vital Force – the Life Energy that quickens us. Third, our worldly beings – our bodies and all related parts – are outlets into the physical world for the Divine flow.

Combining these three realities provides a way of proceeding. We need to claim what is already in us in order to channel this into our lives. We do this by putting on a likeness of God.

Many things enable us to do this: For example, we can wear a smile on the outside, so the Sublime Inner Smile can shine through; walk with a spring in our step so the Lightness of God's Gait can move in ours; soften our hearts so God's Love can melt, brighten, and sweeten everything in us; practise finding joy in everything so that God's Abundance has a place in our lives; and make everything we do a way of creating union, of bringing things together.

In all of this, it is important to make what we do real. Putting on a 'mask', will not enable us to become outlets capable of expressing God fully. Our real capacity for this evolves from our realising true union, joy, love, light, truth ..., not acting out pretend versions. To do this, we practise questing the Divine in everything, in the pleasures and the pains, in the loves and the angers, in the certainties and the fears, in the joys and the losses.

All of Divinity is already in us, and is trying to get into our lives. Acting as if it is already there and then doing what is necessary to make this true is a powerful way of proceeding.

48

Masters

The Wells of Life

Masters are like wells. They are a source of the Water of Life, Water that we all need, if we are to thrive spiritually. We know that they have this capacity from our responses to them when we visit and sit with them. People variously report that they feel as if they are filling up again, becoming enlivened, having a top-up, smoothing out, releasing, dissolving into Light, hearing the Holy Sound, or tasting the Nectar of Life.

Like the surroundings of a well where its water fosters life, the different atmospheres around each Master are soaked with their unique realisations. Their level of Awakening stimulates the same in us. They brighten us with their Lights, they quieten us with their Harmonies, they delight us with their Joy, they sooth us with their Balance and Ease, they sweeten us with their 'Nectarian' Aliveness. We grow in all sorts of ways, nourished by their Love. It is little wonder that people want to spend time with them, time near the well.

When beside a worldly well, we can sit and enjoy the effects on us of the surrounding area, or if we are thirsty, we can drink its water directly. To drink, we need to draw the water. To do this, we need to find and use what is available for that purpose: A bucket, a system of levers, a pump, a tap. Without doing this, we cannot quench our thirst. And every well is different.

To quench our soul thirst by drinking the Water of Life offered by Masters, we need to discover how to get the Water from them. Clearly, only those who can engage with a Master effectively will benefit fully from what he or she offers. Some offer Initiation, some expect service, some teach, some give a hug or touch, some arrange participation in courses or training, and some do it informally through personal contact. Each is different. So it pays to spend time finding out how best to relate to each Master. Fortunately, if we don't find what is required of us with one Master acceptable or palatable enough to act as expected, many others Masters are available.

All the same, it is worth remembering that Masters are scarce resources and to avoid squandering the rare opportunities of knowing them. We will not find true 'Holy Wells' on every street corner. In fact, the modern world is more like a large desert with oases only sparsely scattered through it. Accordingly, when travelling through life, we are wise to take in supplies as and when we can, so we will have enough to get us to the next oasis before we move on again towards our destinations.

It is also worth remembering that Masters are not the Water of Life Itself, they only provide us with access to It. Remember, we will all eventually become our own Divine Wells, provided we do what is necessary – and we do need to do this. At the same time, Masters benefit us enormously: drinking the Living Water through them stimulates Its flow within our own systems.

When eventually we have that flow established inside ourselves, we will no longer need a Master's presence to make it available; we will become our own wells. Yet while no longer needing it, because we are able to quench our soul thirst directly from the Source of Living Water Itself, another Master's flow will remain a delight.

49

Masters

Both Human and Divine

Masters, gurus, avatars and others can become larger than life so very easily. All that is needed is for people to start attributing all sorts of magic to them or exaggerating their reality. People do this in a variety of ways. They may start to worship them, to make up stories about them, to imagine that these extraordinary people are aware of their thoughts, feelings and actions at all times, or that their Masters are ordering their lives. Some people even decide that they should not move, make a decision, think or do even trivial things without first checking their proposed action with their Masters.

In some ways this is a good thing, if the process gets people to relate to their own inner Divinity. However, most people don't seem to take what to a Master is an obvious and crucial next step, a step that would help them to avoid making two very significant mistakes. Their first mistake is to ignore or diminish the Master's own humanity. The second one is to do the same to their own Divinity. Both mistakes are related, as one often feeds the other. And both block direct access to greater realisation.

The reality is that Masters are human beings. They have human bodies and with those bodies come certain qualities and limitations. They usually need to eat, rest, breathe, move their bowels, and release their bladders, and they may become sick, or have accidents. At the same time, many Masters have realised aspects of consciousness or developed abilities that many people have not. Their levels of Realisation seem to take them way beyond normal human abilities. However, by noticing only their 'special capacities' and by failing to notice their humanness, others often block themselves from realising that they, too, could be as these Masters are.

The very fact of a Master's humanness can alert anyone to everyone's potential; for the fact that a Master has realised whatever he or she has automatically shows that others can, too. Unfortunately, putting people on 'divine pedestals' cuts off those who do this from what they could in reality Realise themselves, and what they could in reality do themselves. The pedestals or exaggerations put a Master's Mastery beyond the accomplishment of 'ordinary' people, as far beyond reach as any comparable physical pedestals would place them.

So what is best? Everyone needs to learn to hold two things in his or her awareness: Any signs of Divinity and any signs of humanness, both in themselves and in others, including Masters. Doing so encourages

Divinity in our lives, which then feeds and nurtures our humanness so it can develop to its fullest potential. Divinity and humanness support each other when we do this. By relating to both, by holding both simultaneously in our awareness, we release a wondrous spiritual alchemy that awakens everything to its True Nature – a Nature that is always Divine.

50
Draw Strength
From Within

'I feel so afraid right now with all that's going on in the world. The terrorist attacks have really upset me. I've been shocked, angry, and grief-stricken by turns.' This woman spoke for all present.

'I've seen this many times over the years and it may help us all to talk', said the Master, who was clearly upset himself. 'We feel the way most people do after getting caught in a natural disaster like a fire, flood, or earthquake. Such events can rock us to the core and do so because something fundamental, something on which we have relied has been removed from our lives. It's similar when unexpectedly someone dies, when we lose our jobs, or a partner want to leave. The great variety of reactions we feel at these times is entirely natural'. Many in the group were nodding their heads.

'I just feel so helpless, so swept away with my feelings. I really don't know what to do', said the young woman. The Master replied, 'Yes, of course. Your reactions are both normal and important, and will take you into your

strength if you let them'. He paused, then went on,
'Paradoxically, accepting and living the intensity of
what we experience at these times is the way to claim
our strengths. If we struggle against such experiences,
or try to manage or diminish them, we can find ourselves swept along by them like a twig in a torrent. If,
by contrast, we experience and express what is in us,
then the intensity flows through us, cleansing us, and
energising us for the action we may need to take later.'

After another pause, he continued, 'Of course, a fundamental cause of our extreme reactions to anything is to
do with the way we so often rely on outer stability and
strength to determine our inner stability and strength.
By concentrating too much on the externals in our
lives, we build an unconscious reliance on the mere
props: Our jobs, relationships, homes, personal appearance and so on. From being only props, we thereby
turn them into survival necessities. Then, when they
change, as they commonly do, we feel at the mercy of
external events'. Only a few understood the point and
he knew that they would need time to digest it, so he
added one more comment.

'I repeat: We claim our own strength by experiencing
the full intensity of our feelings. I said this first. My
second point is that there is value in noticing what we
rely on, what we give significance to in our lives. We
need to spend enough time allowing ourselves to experience our responses to these disturbing events, and the
more intense our responses are, the more important

doing this is. People are vulnerable when they don't take enough time for this. By contrast, as we learn to know ourselves deeply through doing this, we increasingly learn to accept our responses to external changes in our lives, whatever those changes are.'

This was a lot to digest and to give his listeners time, the Master fell silent for a while. Then he said, 'Once we have accustomed ourselves to dealing with the levels of intensity that these events stimulate in us, even big changes that cause strong reactions can remain manageable for us. We can remain open to everything, knowing that we can manage ourselves and are capable of contributing constructively to what needs to be done'.

Another pause for more reflection followed, then looking at everyone with great compassion and intensity, the Master added, 'You will note that none of this means that we have to like either the changes to which we are reacting, or the reactions themselves. What it does mean is that we need to practise accepting our responses. Events such as these provide us with ideal opportunities to do so.'

51
Knowledge into Wisdom

'You're completely ignorant', Gerald said, thumping one fist into the other and glaring. 'How dare you teach others before you know what you're doing yourself!' About twenty startled people witnessed this outburst. Without knowing what started it, they were shocked.

Concern replaced shock as the man leapt to his feet and advanced towards the Master and several people immediately and spontaneously moved to protect him. The Master meanwhile seemed unconcerned and, while smiling at his 'adversary', held up a restraining hand in the direction of his 'protectors'. Patting the floor beside him, he said, 'Gerald, I can see you're very upset. Come, sit here, and tell me more'. Completely disarmed by this, Gerald's eyes filled with tears. He flopped next to the Master and sat silently, staring at the floor.

'Whatever it is, you can tell me', the Master coaxed. 'Well', Gerald sniffed remorsefully, 'I went to see another Master the other day'. The Master nodded. 'Lots of people there said that I should follow their Master, that she was the only one worth following, that everyone else was just a "pretend master", pretending

to have knowledge when they were completely ignorant.' He paused, obviously remembering. 'They were
very assertive and persistent.' 'What do you mean
"assertive and persistent"?' the Master enquired.
'Well, they kept it up for ages and shouted at me at
times.' 'Oh, just like you before', the Master's tone was
mildly ironic, 'and that's called being "assertive and
persistent" is it?' Gerald smiled ruefully.

'So what did they want from you?' the Master asked.
'I guess they wanted me to agree with them. They
seemed very upset at all the questions I was asking. I
felt they thought there was only one way and that was
their way. They seemed so convinced and they were
convincing, too.' 'So tell me what they convinced you
of', the master said. 'They convinced me that I should
suspect you and anyone else, except their Master. I
guess I started to doubt you and to believe no one else
could be right.' Smiling, the Master said, 'Yes, good. I
like that. I think it's always a good idea to doubt me
and to keep doubting until you discover the truth for
yourself'.

The Master then looked reflectively at Gerald, who was
now much calmer. 'This is so very common. Lots of
people don't think they can be right, unless they prove
others wrong. They feel uncertain about their own
commitments, so they try to cover this by trying to convince others to "join" with them against everyone else.'
After a short silence, Gerald said uncertainly, 'I think I
see what you mean'.

The Master continued, 'I think everyone can contribute to each of us. Also, I don't think one Master will appeal to everyone, nor have the capacity to help everyone. So, I hope you keep going to this group for as long as you find it helpful. Get all the benefit you can'. Gerald looked very surprised. 'If you stop finding it helpful, stop going. And remember, you are welcome here at any time, whomever else you are visiting.'

The Master meditated briefly before adding, 'I think their enthusiasm is wonderful and they are right in some of what they are claiming. So find where they are right. They just aren't as right as they think they are. And I'm sure that they'll soon temper what they only know partially now; more experience usually turns knowledge into wisdom'.

52
Through 'I Am' to Infinity

'What's the end of all this?' Angelina was somewhat tense as she spoke. 'I've been practising all the things you've taught me for years and it seems like so much to do.' 'What's your point?' the Master asked. 'I guess I'm feeling discouraged' she said. 'After all this time I wonder why I keep meditating and doing all the other things, but then I know why, too. Also, I think it'll take years more, but I want it all now'. The Master scanned her for the deeper need she was expressing, his eyes seeming to become portals into a kind of vastness as he did.

Smiling he said, 'These contradictions show how close you are, how near to the next threshold. Specific meditations and other practices are designed only to get us started on learning the basic skills we will need in order to take the final steps. In the end, however, we need to stop doing all of those things and allow pure awareness to take over. Unless we do, we can't move from body-fulness to body-lessness, from identity to infinity, from diversity to unity, from moments of time to eternity ...' He paused.

'They just sounds like empty words to me. What good are they?' Angelina retorted irritably. 'Well', said the Master, 'the words mean something, but because you're still committed to your worldliness, to body, identity, diversity and time, you don't recognise their value. So, you tell me: What do you need?' She thought for a while, then said, 'Can you give me a taste so I know what you're talking about?'

In answer the Master took her hands in his and closed his eyes. He said softly, 'Keep noticing what you're sitting on for a while and allow yourself to experience whatever happens. Simply let yourself go into it'. Shortly afterwards a soft smile spread from her eyes to her mouth, and a subtle glow surrounded her. She and everyone nearby moved into deep meditative states. Then, after doing whatever he was doing for about five minutes, the Master opened his eyes, gave her hands a little squeeze and let go.

Angelina remained entranced for about half an hour before giving a contented sigh, opening her eyes and looking at him. 'I would've loved that to go on forever', she said. 'My body disappeared into the most wonderfully Loving Light and I was filled with Joy and Peace. I kept letting go and letting go and feeling drawn further back into me all the time. I became one with the aware part of me and with what was happening – everything came together – then even this awareness of Oneness dissolved and I became less and less. I seemed to become Vast Awareness Itself without an observer, although words cannot describe the State I was in.' She paused, a radiant peacefulness surrounding her, then added, 'It was amazing'.

'Wonderful!' said the Master. 'And notice how there is nothing to do in that final experience. Everything simply is. Yet, in the beginning you probably needed to keep encouraging yourself to stay aware of what you were sitting on, to let go and to stay with the dissolving. This 'doing' enables us to move directly into being "I AM". "I AM" is a state of Oneness with Experience in which the observer has expanded to include all that is, while at the same time having nothing but the merest vestige of "I-ness" in it. Through "I AM" we move into the Vast Nothingness of Infinity. Only there do everything and nothing combine so that all polarities dissolve into a State beyond description.'

53

Digest the Soup, Don't Fight in It

Two people began to argue passionately. The others in
the room were startled. It was very unusual for people
to make a commotion while the Master was meditating.
They tried to hush the two combatants, who, nevertheless, continued without a pause.

'What are you doing?' someone whispered angrily,
'You'll disturb the Master'. 'What do you mean, "What
are we doing?"' one of them hissed back, 'Mind your
own business!'

'What are you all doing?' a voice said, its serenity a powerful command to pay attention. 'You're all so upset –
and for what? That you might disturb me? We have far
more important things to deal with right now.' He
paused to claim their full attention, then added, 'Your
anger and agitation are coming from those very things'.
They looked puzzled and there was a long silence.

'The dogs of war are straining at their leashes, snarling
at real or imagined adversaries and determined to do

135

the job they think themselves trained to do. Their handlers, the politicians, seem intent to loose them on their assumed foes. There is talk of war all around us. TV and the other news media are filled with it, speculating about it, exciting people about it – selling their services through it. And, movies, TV programs and stories are increasingly war-like, their strategies more ruthless; caring for people as human beings is subsiding under claims that almost anything is allowable in the name of expediency. "We are fighting a war/terrorism/evil and we have to do things we don't like doing", they say.' By this time the Master seemed to radiate a great force that his quiet intensity was carrying into the hearts of all there. Again he paused.

'The practical result of all of this is that the world is currently bathed in a violent atmosphere created from acts of violence, passionate talk of violence, preparations for violence, justifications for violence made in advance of the acts and, importantly, people living in fear of violence. One result is what we just witnessed. People who normally would not get angry are getting angry; people who would normally get angry are getting angrier – and both are feeling justified in doing so.' Many present were nodding with new understanding now, having felt this themselves.

'We are all in this soup and to change it we need to digest it, not thrash around in it. In other words, open up to the atmosphere, let it penetrate you, let your system absorb it. But do not act it out. Instead, allow it to

stimulate you as your digest it through staying aware of
the physical things and events in your immediate vicinity. Also, think accepting thoughts and concentrate on
the real resolution to real problems. Encourage feelings
of gratitude and joy. Act in ways that bring people
together, that protect the vulnerable, that respect aliveness in all. Let your peace bring peace to the world by
persisting in this way. It is crucial that we all do this at
this time and it will work, provided we do.'

54
Like An Eagle in Flight

It was a sultry spring afternoon. High, billowing storms clouds had threatened for hours. As if reflecting the mood of the day, one of the people near the Master was agitated and seemed unable to settle. He had been talking about how the turbulence of his life seemed to prevent him from meditating regularly and how, when he did meditate, he was 'all over the place' inside. The Master had listened attentively without saying much at the time. He seemed content to sit in silence.

Some time afterwards, the first of several thunderstorms broke. Brilliant lighting forked through the sky, hitting lighting conductors on the tops of nearby buildings. The deafening, instantaneous crack of thunder and the pungent hiss of nature's discharging electricity were testaments to how powerful the storm was and how close. Everyone except the Master jumped with fright. Then pelting rain began to fall, drowning out all other sound as it deluged the roof and nearby ground. Wind swirled and gusted strongly, picking up all it could and carrying it away. And the natural light faded – everything seemed to become lost in turbulent greyness.

Then, as quickly as it had arrived, the storm was gone.
The sun shone again, everything smelled sweet and
fresh, and the atmosphere, while still hot and humid,
was distinctly more comfortable and soothing. The
respite lasted only a short time, however, before
another storm marched through the area. Almost a
repeat of the first, the manifest power of nature was
startling and exciting.

As the second storm passed on, the Master looked up
attentively and became transfixed by something outside the window. Eventually he sighed and said,
'Look at that. Someone has been listening so beautifully'. Waving his hand in the direction of the young
man who had been talking earlier, the Master said,
'There's the answer to your question about
turbulence'.

They all looked out to see an eagle hawk high in the
sky, buffeted both by strong updrafts and winds gusting
from different directions. Yet amazingly it was somehow managing to stay in exactly the same spot within
the frame created by the window, as if somehow pinned
there. To achieve this feat, its wings were constantly at
work, making quick adjustments, both major and
minor. Looking at the action of the wings alone, it
seemed impossible that it could stay stationary, yet it
was. The bird's constant position in relation to the
window frame clearly showed its poise, balance and
persistence in holding to its direction and intention in
the face of incredible turbulence.

'Think of what you are witnessing', said the Master, pointing at the bird. 'That's the mastery we all need in order to ride the currents, eddies and blasting gusts of life; that's how we need to allow life's events to flow past us and, in the midst of everything, to keep our poise. We need to keep our eyes on the goal; to keep heading for where we want to go; always finding a way of getting there, no matter what is happening in our immediate vicinity.'

With that, the eaglehawk was gone, soaring high into the sky. The Master laughed delightedly and pointed again, 'Then, as the bird just did, when we are ready, we will move forward and up, soaring to the heights to find that Sublime Nourishment is within our reach'. To the young man, he said, 'So next time you are feeling turbulent, imitate that bird. Use the message it came here to give you today'.

55
Dappled Dawn of Awakening

'Oh you're always so positive and optimistic about everything.' The man glowered at the Master. 'Life just isn't like that. But all you ever talk about is concentrating on love and life and joy and harmony and things like that. I get so angry with you. Life is filled with pain and distress and anger and ... and all sorts of things. And all your weak-wristed stuff just doesn't help.'

'I can see that you do get angry', the Master replied neutrally as he looked around at all present. Some seemed shocked at the man's outburst. The Master, by contrast, was completely at ease as he went on. 'And I know it seems contradictory in some ways. But, in my experience, what I teach is by far the fastest way to progress and ...', at this he paused at length, just looking evenly at the man, then he continued, 'you've missed the point of what I've been teaching you.' The subject of his look blanched momentarily, then, mustering more passion, glared again at the Master.

Still completely unaffected by the man's performance, the Master said. 'Let's go through my approach one step at a time. First, I usually suggest that we give attention to what we want or need, no matter what we are experiencing, because in that way we will end up with what we want or need rather than something else. At the same time, I also suggest that we live the experience of each moment, live it fully, no matter what it is. Much of the time, these experiences may be very pleasing to us, but at other times they may include extremes of rage, terror, grief, agony or other milder discomforts. There is no avoidance in this, if we are to experience what it there, and there is no easy way to do it cither. To embrace such feelings and the contraction that goes with them demands great courage, determination and commitment. However, the point is, too, that we'll resolve such experiences much more quickly, if – and this is very important – in the midst of the anguish and distress we experience, we quest for and keep some attention on how we would like things to be.' He paused to let this sink in. Some people were nodding and the man was looking both calmer and a little shaken.

The Master continued, 'Second, one of the values of taking this approach is that our systems soften and open up when we concentrate on experiences like love, pleasure, joy, wonder, gratitude, happiness and the like. This concentration releases us from the contractions of our bodies, of feeling and of thinking that our previous holding and withholding have produced. With the release, with the expansion and opening, out comes all that we have held onto'. Again he looked at the man, this time with firmness. 'At that point, you will then have the job of living through even greater discomfort and distress than even you might imagine, for this approach brings everything to the surface so much more intensely and quickly than your way does.'

He paused for emphasis. 'As a result, the path I teach is actually far harder in many ways that others – not easier. True Life is filled with Light, Joy, Love, Silence, Peace, Sweetness and Fragrance, and our day-to-day lives often only approximate this. That they are approximations doesn't make me wrong, however; it's a matter of what will work best. My goal is for you to learn to live Life as fully and as quickly as you can. And this is why I recommend what I do. However, I have never asserted or pretended that it is a path bathed only with Light. Rest assured: The Awakening process is a very dappled dawning indeed, at least in the beginning'.

56
Light in the Dark

'Misery – overwhelming, unremitting, grinding, dark and crushing – hammered at me. I could feel it in my bowels, in the cells of my body, in my head and arms and legs, as if I was surrounded by it, submerged in it, awash with it. Dull greyness flattening all views, dull sounds echoing through hollow emptiness, dull feelings erasing all hope, dull fragrance and essence swirling poisoned foulness into everything – and on and on and on it went with its own seemingly unstoppable momentum. All feeling, all thought was carried in its currents, inexorably swallowing me in its dark vortex. The power of it all was astounding, with me riven in a kind of helplessness, having fantasies of needing to end it, with an unutterable inevitability as part of the loss of aliveness and of all hope that anything like aliveness could ever return.' The Master stopped talking, clearly touched again by what he had experienced. 'This was part of my path and may be a part of yours at some stage, too.'

Those around were sitting shocked, in tears, wide-eyed, or fidgeting uncomfortably. Unspoken questions hung

in the air, 'What did you do? How did you deal with
it?' Nodding as if actually hearing the questions, the
Master looked around and went on. 'I deliberately sat
with my experience, embraced it, lived it. I allowed it
to take me over, wondering if I could ever survive such
overwhelming intensity, such a loss of contact with
Life, Aliveness, Confidence, Light, Harmony and
Sweetness. Gone – all Life was gone – or at least it
seemed so.'

He shifted position as he spoke, seeming to be uncomfortable. 'All I had left was my practice – and I clung to
it. Then that failed and I clung to the memory that it
had worked before – in, by then, what felt like a very
distant the past. All I knew to do was to concentrate,
to concentrate deeply and fully on the bodily part of
what I was going through – and this is what I did.
Doing this was my lifeline. Doing it was excruciating.
And it was doing it led me back to Life.

'The day was overcast, with a deep, hovering greyness
that exactly matched my mood. Then, unexpectedly,
after what seemed like an eternity, something caught
my attention outside my window. It was a speck of
light. No sooner had I seen it than it was gone again,
leaving me looking for where it had been. Back to my
body I went; taking my attention there, I continued to
live the ebb and flow of my murky tides, the tensions,
the pain, the holding and my "stuckness" … Suddenly,
the sparkling speck was back, this time for a little
larger – a tiny light in the darkness. Then, after an

accidental shift in my position to the right changed its colour, I quickly discovered that further movement took the light speck through the whole colour spectrum. By going back to my body again, even as I experimented, I unexpectedly turned the speck into a tiny, radiant mandala, with filigrees of rainbow light shining and sparkling at me. At this point, I became aware that the arrival of my tiny light had changed my inner world. It, too, now had a spark of light. So the external light became my beacon, and something else to experience in my body in the small hope that it would expand inside me.

'Very soon, and very unexpectedly, sunlight illuminated the ground on which my outer light still glimmered and shimmered, and I felt my spirits lift some more. Then, wonder of wonders, with a flicker of movement, a beautiful bird with a very pointed, slightly curved beak appeared, its bright yellow plumage surrounded by white, brown and dark blue-black. A small honeyeater, it set about nourishing itself on the flowers I could see in the bright sunlight that now bathed everything, including my still-shining small mandala of light. And by then, I was alive once more, nourished by the renewal of the Life I could feel in everything.'

The Master stopped reflectively, then added, 'I realised, yet again, that there's always Light in any of the darkness we experience in our lives. We simply need to hold to our practice to discover that it is indeed always there'.

57
Petal on Pond

'What can I do?' a lively young woman asked the Master. 'I tell people what they need to do to meditate and to follow what you teach, but they don't do it. They just don't seem to get it. And the more I tell them to do it in the way I can see they need to, the less they seem to follow through.' The Master smiled encouragingly, recognising the woman's good-heartedness. 'I think you're trying too hard', he said.

'Great gentleness, tenderness and delicacy are needed when we make contact with others. We need to have immense respect for them. At times, tough approaches are needed, of course; people who are struggling, conflicted, aggressive, or deeply withdrawn may need strength, vigour, intensity or even flaring clarity in order for us to reach them. This is because their own intensity blocks their consciousness at those times.' The woman nodded vigorously as the Master spoke, thinking that she understood perfectly and that he was agreeing with her. The Master continued, 'Even then, though, this way of approaching others is best done as a matching or balancing of forces. It's best done with the goal of communicating, not to try to control, over-power, abuse, or hurt.'

'Think about it this way', the Master continued after another pause. 'Ideally, we need to make contact with others with such delicacy that we cause barely a ripple, perhaps not even that. The more we disturb them, the more people are likely to react against what we do, rather than embrace it. It's as if we need to approach others with the same care that we would have to take when putting a flower petal onto the surface of a mirror-smooth pond without causing a ripple. This requires great respect, great delicacy, great dexterity, great acceptance, great love and great appreciation.'

The young woman nodded, this time, with real under-standing, 'Hmm, I see why people have pushed back at me now; I've been pushing them.' 'With the best of intentions, I can see', the Master responded, smiling warmly and touching her hand affectionately. 'Now think about something else. What we do with others, we're always doing with ourselves in some way. So I'm sure you're just as forthright, instructional and demanding with yourself as with the others you have mentioned. Is that so?' 'Yes, it is', she answered, with a rueful look in his direction. 'And this is something you do during meditation, as well?' he conjectured. She was remained silent for a short time, then replied reflectively, 'Hmm – yes I think it is'.

'Well, when you sit in meditation, remember to treat your experiences as I've just recommended you treat other people. Instead of trying to make your experiences conform, to boss them into alignment with your expectations, approach them carefully, respectfully and with full acceptance. Embrace them, cherish them and realise their delicate, vulnerable, exquisite beauty and power. Practise matching them, touching them lightly and letting them touch you lightly, too. Remember your intent as "Place a petal on a pond", not "Do what I tell you!" By joining your experiences with care and delicacy, they will open to you and welcome you, rather than react against you.' 'Yes, I see, I understand now. I'll do that.' The Master smiled again.

58
Raft in Troubled Waters

'Once a long time ago, I imagined writing to my Masters to communicate the significance of what they had done for me and to thank them adequately. This was a seemingly impossible task at the time.' The Master looked around the small group of people to whom he was talking. 'I am glad to say that I'm in a better position to do it these days.' 'What would you say now?' someone asked.

Looking off into the distance the Master started to speak. 'You gave me a voice when I could not speak and filled that voice with words so that I could express the previously inexpressible: My doubts and fears, my hopes and then, increasingly as you guided me towards and into Life, my joys, my wonder at the Beauty of Life, my love for all things, my curiosity, my delight in the release of Life into life, my awe – everything.

'You helped me to see what I could not see, to see what was real and what was not, and to see that I had been blinded to Real Life. Then, as my vision cleared, you helped me to see how I was creating a world filled with dark shadows, loss and dejection. You helped me to

learn to celebrate the beauty of a new world, a
Shimmering, Wondrous Paradise, incandescent with
Divine Light.

'When I was drowning in my own delusional commitments to pain and sorrow and resentment and worry,
you gave me your hands, not to pull me out – oh no, that
would not have worked – but to keep me feeling safe
enough for long enough to stay and to learn that my
dclusions held no real risk. Your hands on mine infused
me with a living essence that nourished me at my very
roots in a way I had never experienced before. This
essence released me from my delusions and opened me
to the Real. Your hands on mine offered me to Life,
much as loving fathers and mothers offer their sons and
daughters to their Destinies in the Divine, with full confidence that those Divine Destinies hold all that their
children will ever need. What blessings these are!

'You were the raft I clung to during the storms of my
life. Initially I felt you only as a way of staying afloat,
though gradually I realised that you were offering very
much more. As your Love transformed me, enlivened
me, released me from my own contraction and commitment to contraction; because your Love's first touch
alerted me to something different, then seeped into me
and finally swamped me by making me one with It; I
came to my Self by Realising something we all have and
can come to know. Life, God, Love, the Infinite, the
Void – call It whatever you will – in all Its "Is-ness",
this is all there is – and nothing more is necessary.

'Because you Loved me, stayed with me, saw me through to the end, because you Spoke to me, in silence and in words, because you Guided me, redirecting my attention when I was fixated and limited, opening me to the Real Ease and Wonder and Joy of Aliveness; because you took the time again and again and again, because you accepted me as me, no matter what, no matter what I thought of myself; because of all these things and very much more, I am who I am today. Because you Loved me, because you Enfolded me, allowing me to Dissolve in You, I now Know the Reality of Me, the Reality of the Love that you Live – and I know "I AM" that Love, too.

'I thank you all and celebrate with you from the very Essence of my Being.'

59
And We Become One

'I've always wondered what you do during darshan. It's such a wonderful, loving experience for me', an older man in the group said. Everyone was immediately interested, many of them having wanted to ask the Master about this, too. 'I'm also curious about what it's like for you', the man added to accompanying nods from several others.

'Well, these are much easier questions to ask, than the answers are easy to give.' The Master looked around, remembering some of his experiences with each of the people present. 'It's different with each of you and different each time, too. Nonetheless, I'll see if I can explain.' He paused, then went on. 'As each of you approaches me, my system starts to prepare for you, even before I've finished with the person already with me. Sometimes I'm aware of these adjustments, sometimes not.

'As you arrive, I clear myself from what I've just done with the person ahead of you and meditate briefly, linking myself to the Divine and affirming, as I do, that what we share will be ideal for us both. Once you are

153

settled, I usually reach out to you and touch you physically in some way, though not always. Sometimes I simply experience your energy without any contact; sometimes I use my eyes; sometimes my ears. I can also link with you through my thoughts, feelings or intention.

'Once we are linked, I sit and await developments. I allow you to affect me in whatever way you do; I don't try to control or manipulate this in any way. I simply sit, remaining as open to you and as available to you as I can – and I await the outcome. I cultivate complete acceptance in myself of all that I experience while I do this. If you haven't already, at this point you're likely to experience me as accepting you completely. And as I cultivate this complete acceptance within myself, I bathe us both in Love.

'My Loving you, my openness to you and your availability to me can automatically produce a Wondrous Union, a coming together into a shared field of Light, Love, Peace and Understanding. We know deep, intimate sharing. I know your Essence and join with you through that knowing. Divine Grace is an obvious presence in the midst of this Oneness; it is always there, always creating its magic – a magic, by the way, that occurs from our being this Grace without our doing anything. We coexist with each other, seemingly suspended out of time and space for an eternity, although in worldly time it is only a few moments. During this phase, I open myself even more fully to the

Divine.' The Master paused, radiant and alive, obviously meditating what he had just described.

'My whole worldly experience of this, which by then is of some level of Oneness with you, is distilled, clarified, purified and harmonised in the Divine. Direct knowing shows me these changes as they occur – contraction releases, light becomes brighter and more transparent, healing occurs, deep peace and inner silence emerge – and much more. All the while, I physically and in other ways do what I seem prompted to do with you or to say to you.'

The Master smiled reflectively, then with a twinkle in his eyes, said, 'In summary, I take you into my Self and digest us both. Hmmm, very nice we are, too!'

60
Receiving Darshan
(by Kathryn Schofield)

Each night, during a seven-day workshop in which
everyone was silent for all but one brief session per day,
all participants were offered nightly, silent darshan
with Ken and Elizabeth. I'd had beautiful and remark-
able experiences with them on many other such occa-
sions and knew that these times always contributed to
my awakening. All the same, I was so moved after one
experience with Ken during this particular workshop,
that I wanted specially to share it with him. I wrote
the following.

'I kneel and wait beside the Master. The person ahead
of me will soon be gone. I raise my eyes to observe his
blessing. Soft white light emanates from his Beloved
Face. Such gentleness, such strength, such Love.

'My turn comes. I move towards him, my heart pounding
as I go more deeply into his field of Grace. I kneel before
him in surrender. He reaches out and touches me.

'I have come home.

'His light enfolds me with shimmering intensity and I know my present point of power. As he touches me with loving strength, I feel my heart dissolve in white fire. This moment is eternal. We merge in endless, timeless Bliss.

'The Master lightly squeezes my hands with definite intention, his signal that physically it is time for me to move away.

'As I leave him, I realise that we, as with all things, are in eternal Darshan: On-going Divine Union, each with each; and that this earthly, physical blessing is a portal to what lies beyond.

'When sitting back in my own place again, I resonate and shine with Life and Light. Everything is clear to me and I know that through the guidance of his blessing, the Master brings me home to God.'

Biame
NETWORK

Biame Network is an international, non-profit, educational organisation. An Incorporated Association with members in many countries, it was founded in 1984 by Ken and Elizabeth Mellor. Its primary purpose is to take a spiritually-based approach to life that enables people to live in ways that promote Awakening. The approach, called Urban Mysticism, is down-to-earth, practical and easy to use. Its practices come from sources in both the East and the West, and integrate them all. Anyone living in the modern world can use it.

The network's approach is broad, taking in virtually all aspects of life. In particular, it emphasises practical living skills, parenting and child rearing, couple development, relationship management, self-management in daily life at home and work, practical meditations, specific spiritual practices, personal and spiritual mentoring, and Reiki healing and training.

Anyone interested is encouraged to contact the network. Most of the organisation's activities are open to everyone, whatever their race, spiritual or religious orientations, ethnic origins, age, gender or gender preferences. Some activities, such as the network's training program, are available only to people selected in response to personal applications. Anyone can apply.

Both regular and one-off courses, and workshop programs are offered in various parts of the world. The
training program acts as a venue for systematic learning for people interested in developing and evolving
personally, or for those wanting to participate in the
many activities the network fosters. In addition, Biame
Network has an ever-expanding range of teaching and
learning materials available. You can look at the
Website or contact the office directly, I you have any
enquiries.

All enquiries are welcome and can be directed to:

Biame Network Inc.
PO Box 271
Seymour
Victoria 3661
Australia
Tel.: + 61 3 5799 1198
Fax.: + 61 3 5799 1132
Email: biamenet@eck.net.au
Website: www.biamenetwork.net